ROUTLEDGE LIBRARY EDITIONS: VIRGINIA WOOLF

Volume 4

VIRGINIA WOOLF AND THE POETRY OF FICTION

VIRGINIA WOOLF AND THE POETRY OF FICTION

STELLA MCNICHOL

LONDON AND NEW YORK

First published in 1990 by Routledge

This edition first published in 2018
by Routledge
2 Park Square, Milton Park, Abingdon, Oxon OX14 4RN

and by Routledge
711 Third Avenue, New York, NY 10017

Routledge is an imprint of the Taylor & Francis Group, an informa business

© 1990, Stella McNichol

All rights reserved. No part of this book may be reprinted or reproduced or utilised in any form or by any electronic, mechanical, or other means, now known or hereafter invented, including photocopying and recording, or in any information storage or retrieval system, without permission in writing from the publishers.

Trademark notice: Product or corporate names may be trademarks or registered trademarks, and are used only for identification and explanation without intent to infringe.

British Library Cataloguing in Publication Data
A catalogue record for this book is available from the British Library

ISBN: 978-1-138-54104-7 (Set)
ISBN: 978-1-351-01117-4 (Set) (ebk)
ISBN: 978-0-8153-5933-3 (Volume 4) (hbk)
ISBN: 978-1-351-12050-0 (Volume 4) (ebk)

Publisher's Note
The publisher has gone to great lengths to ensure the quality of this reprint but points out that some imperfections in the original copies may be apparent.

Disclaimer
The publisher has made every effort to trace copyright holders and would welcome correspondence from those they have been unable to trace.

VIRGINIA WOOLF AND THE POETRY OF FICTION

STELLA McNICHOL

ROUTLEDGE
LONDON AND NEW YORK

First published 1990
by Routledge
11 New Fetter Lane, London EC4P 4EE
29 West 35th Street, New York, NY 10001

© 1990 Stella McNichol

Disk conversion and typesetting by
Ponting–Green Publishing Services, London
Printed in Great Britain by
T.J. Press, Padstow, Cornwall

All rights reserved. No part of this book may be reprinted or
reproduced or utilized in any form or by any electronic, mechanical,
or other means, now known or hereafter invented, including photocopying and recording, or in any information storage or retrieval
system, without permission in writing from the publishers.

British Library Cataloguing in Publication Data
McNichol, Stella,
  Virginia Woolf and the poetry of fiction.
  1. Fiction in English. Woolf, Virginia –
  Critical studies
  I. Title
  823'.912

Library of Congress Cataloging in Publication Data
McNichol, Stella.
  Virginia Woolf and the poetry of fiction.

  Bibliography: p.
  Includes index.
  1. Woolf, Virginia, 1882–1941—Criticism and interpretation. I.
Title.
PR6045.072Z8155 1990 823'.912 88–26392

ISBN 0–415–00329–6

FOR TOM

CONTENTS

	Acknowledgements	ix
	A note on the texts	x
	Introduction	xi
1	SYMBOLIC INTRUSIONS IN *THE VOYAGE OUT*	1
2	'SHAPING FANTASIES' IN *NIGHT AND DAY*	16
3	THE POETIC NARRATIVE OF *JACOB'S ROOM*	39
4	THE RHYTHMIC ORDER OF *MRS. DALLOWAY*	62
5	*TO THE LIGHTHOUSE*: AN ELEGY	91
6	*THE WAVES*: A PLAYPOEM	117
7	THE 'PURE POETRY' OF *BETWEEN THE ACTS*	141
	Select bibliography	175
	Index	181

ACKNOWLEDGEMENTS

What I have written about Virginia Woolf's fiction in the following pages is derived from my reading of the fiction itself and of Virginia Woolf's non-fictional writings, in particular her diaries. I am aware of what has been written on her life, her career as a writer, and her fiction, and from such studies I have derived much stimulation. My own approach to Virginia Woolf's fiction, however, does not depend on any of them in such a particular way as to require footnote acknowledgement, nor have I thought it desirable to interrupt the attention of readers by directing them to topics outside the immediate scope of my study.

My thanks are due to Quentin Bell for continued helpfulness over a long period of time. I am grateful to the Humanities Research Committee of Lancaster University for enabling me to take two terms of leave while writing this book.

The author and publishers wish to thank the Virginia Woolf Literary Estate, The Hogarth Press and Harcourt Brace Jovanovich, Inc., for permission to reproduce extracts from Virginia Woolf's writings.

A NOTE ON THE TEXTS

With the exception of *Night and Day* (Duckworth), all references to the text of Virginia Woolf's novels are to the Hogarth Press Uniform Edition. The novel under discussion in each chapter is referred to by page number only, and other works by abbreviated titles.

The following abbreviations have been used:

VO	*The Voyage Out*
ND	*Night and Day*
JR	*Jacob's Room*
MD	*Mrs. Dalloway*
TL	*To the Lighthouse*
W	*The Waves*
Y	*The Years*
BA	*Between the Acts*
AROO	*A Room of One's Own*
AWD	*A Writer's Diary*
CE I–IV	*Collected Essays*
CR	*The Common Reader*
MB	*Moments of Being*
Bell I, II	Quentin Bell, *Virginia Woolf: a Biography*

Full details of these works are given in the bibliography.

INTRODUCTION

Oscar Wilde's brilliant, if unfair, epigram at Browning's expense – 'Meredith is a prose Browning, and so is Browning. He used poetry as a medium for writing in prose' – was a criticism both of the content and of the form of his poetry. To claim that Virginia Woolf is a poet who used prose fiction as her medium – the argument of the present study – is likewise to assert something both about the content and about the form of her novels. Often she has the cadences, sometimes even the rhymes, associated with lyric poetry:

> So on a summer's day
> the waves collect, overbalance, and fall;
> collect and fall;...
>
> ...
> that is all.
>
> (*MD*: 44–5)

Taking the term poetry in a more general sense, it can be shown that the imagery and the structure of her novels arise from a creative imagination that is profoundly poetic in nature. This is not, therefore, a stylistic study of the fiction of Virginia Woolf; or one which focuses narrowly on the lyric qualities of her writing. It does, however, focus on a specific poetic quality or aspect in each novel under discussion as a starting point for interpretation.

The first two chapters of this study indicate some of the ways in which poetic features intrude into the text of what is generally described as a traditional novel. In the case of *The Voyage Out*, for instance, occurrences and events as mundane as a dance and a picnic, ordinary episodes in the chronological

INTRODUCTION

sequence of events, take on a symbolic dimension which adds a further layer of meaning to that conveyed by the naturally unfolding plot. In *Night and Day* there is a move into fantasy as the central characters embark on a quest which takes them into a world of psychological confusion in which they learn to distinguish between dream and reality. The poetic aspect of this novel inheres mainly in its Shakespearean parallels. *Jacob's Room* is more experimental than the two novels that preceded it. It is Virginia Woolf's most theoretical work, yet even here meaning is conveyed poetically. First there is the dual movement of the novel whereby the optimistic thrust of the central character is undermined by the elegiac voice of the narrator, and second there is the way in which poetic connections are made between the episodes as images and motifs become interwoven into the fabric of meaning. These three novels contain writing of considerable sophistication and maturity.

The major fiction is approached in a more narrowly specific way: *Mrs. Dalloway* through its poetic rhythms, *To the Lighthouse* as a multi-perspectival exploration of a reality embodied in a single image, and *The Waves* as a playpoem. A new kind of poetry is to be found in the last novel.

The aspects of the poetic that constitute the different approaches to each novel in this study indicate something of the way in which Virginia Woolf altered her method as she developed from novel to novel, her method being dictated by different preoccupations.

The first novels are all about young people growing up in Edwardian England. The third of these moves further forward in time: Jacob Flanders dies in the Great War at the age of twenty-six. The second phase is that of the psychological novel. Virginia Woolf's most truly psychological novel is *Mrs. Dalloway*. It is significant that her Modernist manifesto, the essay 'Modern Fiction', was published in the same year. In this essay she expresses her commitment to an inward-looking fiction, recognizes the potential of the stream of consciousness technique (though she does not use that term), and sees that it is necessary to invent new narrative structures to reflect new insights into life. In her progression from *Mrs. Dalloway* to *The Waves* the emphasis of her concern shifts from the psychological to the mystical, the titles of the books reflecting that develop-

INTRODUCTION

ment: having explored and expressed psychological reality she moves beyond the human to the universal and cosmic reality that she from time to time glimpses as 'a fin in the waste of waters'. The novels of this period reflect the mood of England in the 1920s. The central characters are now middle-aged.

Virginia Woolf wrote two novels of the 1930s, *The Years*, a novel of realism, and the poetic novel *Between the Acts*. They reflect the mood of England in the decade that saw the Depression and the rise of Fascism, and that concluded with the outbreak of war. The bias of her late work is social and historical, and the central characters are elderly. Having plumbed the depths of the human psyche and explored the capacity of the individual to transcend time and the routine dailiness of life, Virginia Woolf turns outwards in her late fiction to consider his situation and significance in the continuum of history. *Between the Acts* has a time span (if one includes the pageant) of 500 years. The focus of this novel is on our consciousness of history whereby the self and history are interlocked in an evolving system. The self of the present assumes the past.

The aim of this study, as the above suggests, is to move away from the general view of Virginia Woolf as a psychological novelist. All such considerations focus on the novels of her central period whereby the early novels are viewed dismissively as apprenticeship works, and those she wrote after *The Waves* as novels of decline. This view fails to do justice to her overall achievement as a novelist. In focusing on the poetic rather than the psychological features of her fiction it is possible in some measure to do justice to its greater range and variety.

xiii

Chapter One

SYMBOLIC INTRUSIONS IN
THE VOYAGE OUT

The Voyage Out, written between 1907 and 1913 and published in 1915, reflects the mood and spirit of the Edwardian period. Through its central story the theme of love and marriage is explored, and through, in particular, the emergence of a young woman from the confines of a restrictive Victorian household into a freer world of the 'New Woman', the theme of the changing social role of women is opened up.

This first novel by a writer of sophisticated 'Modernist' fiction is a traditional novel and a *bildungsroman*, and as such it has been too readily dismissed by critics for not being innovative. Yet it is only its surface that makes it a novel of realism, and only at the surface of the book that the genre of the *bildungsroman* is truly applicable. *The Voyage Out* is a novel of surface simplicity, and of submerged complexity. Central to the surface realism of the traditional novel, and of the *bildungsroman* in particular, is the story of Rachel Vinrace who develops out of immaturity and ignorance into womanhood through a series of encounters and events. These chiefly consist of a sea journey and a river journey, social events (the picnic and the dance in particular), sexual awakening, and falling in love and engagement to be married, all of which form the novel's linear structure. Within that structure the theme of love and marriage is examined in a widening social context. A strong sense of social change and disruption is built into the narrative, and the period, the Edwardian era, is specified by the particularity of the novel's documentation.

The development of Rachel Vinrace is central to all levels of *The Voyage Out*'s structure. Virginia Woolf explores Rachel's feelings, traces the development of her mind, and above all

1

charts the fluctuations of her awakening consciousness. She traces her psychological development through the events which shape the course of her life and in which relationships develop, and these events are balanced by instances of solitary reflection and introspection. It is particularly by the fusion of the deeper symbolic structure of the novel into the natural sequence of events dictated by the plot structure that Virginia Woolf achieves a narrative of distinction. The events, because they are infused with the imaginative force of poetry, take on a mythic quality, and they linger in the mind.

The first of the significant events to take place is the picnic on Monte Rosa organized by Terence Hewet. Rachel's invitation to join the party is brought to her by her aunt who interrupts a moment of introspection. That moment is one in which the author analyses the way in which Rachel learns about life vicariously through what she reads, then, more significantly, examines the kind of mental processes that underlie the simple act of taking up a book, reading it for a while, and then discarding it. Helen had promised her a room of her own 'cut off from the rest of the house, large and private ... a fortress as well as a sanctuary'. Within her 'fortress' Rachel had been reading Ibsen (after that it was Meredith's *Diana of the Crossways*: she chooses to read 'modern books').

Rachel's experience of reading the play goes through different stages. First she becomes the heroine (Nora in *A Doll's House*) and lives the part for several days. Next comes the stage of personal enrichment from the experience. The author conveys Rachel's direct experience of imaginative life in reading by describing the way in which she responds to her surroundings: as she puts her book down,

[t]he landscape outside, because she had seen nothing but print for the space of two hours, now appeared amazingly solid and clear, but although there were men on the hill washing the trunks of olive trees with a white liquid, for the moment she herself was the most vivid thing in it – an heroic statue in the middle of the foreground, dominating the view. Ibsen's plays always left her in that condition.

(143)

SYMBOLIC INTRUSIONS IN *THE VOYAGE OUT*

The extraordinary nature of the experience, the heightening of the human consciousness, is presented in visual terms in the image of the 'heroic statue'. When the transition from the imaginative world to the real world has been completed, Rachel attains the third level of mentally questioning the significance of what she has read.

She finds *Diana of the Crossways* less satisfactory. After putting the book aside, she sits immobile in a distracted state of mind. Here Virginia Woolf builds into a passage of ordinary narration an account of the existential experience of self-awareness. After the effort of concentration required by her reading, Rachel lets her mind relax. She gradually begins to take note of sounds around her; they form themselves into a regular rhythm. As that rhythm begins to assert itself in her consciousness, she senses the strangeness of life, but in a detached way: 'It was all very real, very big, very impersonal...'(144). In order to bring herself back to a sense of her own personality she goes through various self-conscious actions in which she looks upon herself, or at aspects of her self, as something separate from herself and so observable in an objective manner:

> after a moment or two she began to raise her first finger and let it fall on the arm of her chair so as to bring back to herself some consciousness of her own existence.
>
> (144)

Once she is 'self-possessed' again, she notes through reference to ordinary objects around her the extraordinary nature of her own human existence, and then in and through that the nature of existence itself. This transcendent experience takes over her consciousness again: this is indicated by her sense of being on a plane of existence outside or beyond her body ('She could not raise her finger any more.... She forgot that she had any fingers to raise'(145)).

Rachel's experience of being suspended in time, in existence, on two different planes at once is conveyed unobtrusively within the simple surface narration of what is happening to her:

> The things that existed were so immense and so desolate.... She continued to be conscious of these vast

VIRGINIA WOOLF AND THE POETRY OF FICTION

masses of substance for a long stretch of time, the clock still ticking in the midst of the universal silence.

(145)

The one word 'universal' indicates a different experiential mode within the mundane and the tangible. This is a fairly early (1915) expression in literature of the Bergsonian distinction between two different kinds of time, the 'clock' time of everyday finite existence and the 'durée' of psychological time in which the mind is momentarily freed from the shackles of the temporal to experience infinity or that which is beyond time. The nature of time, and the relation between past and present and future, is explored with greater complexity in Virginia Woolf's later novels. What she says is essentially very similar to what T. S. Eliot examines through his image of the 'still point' and in 'the point of intersection of the timeless with time' (*Four Quartets*). He tends towards the philosophic in the expression of the theme in his poetry; Virginia Woolf tends increasingly towards the poetic ('flowers of darkness', 'buds on the tree of life' – *MD*: 33) in her psychological and phenomenological explorations of it in her fiction. In this particular instance Rachel's heightened awareness is interrupted by Mrs Ambrose's arrival with the invitation to join the expedition to go up Monte Rosa. The tone of the novel of realism is in this way carefully preserved, as Rachel seems momentarily unable to adjust to the intrusion:

> "Come in," she said mechanically, for a string in her brain seemed to be pulled by a persistent knocking at the door....
>
> The utter absurdity of a woman coming into a room with a piece of paper in her hand amazed Rachel....
>
> For the second time Rachel read the letter, but to herself. This time, instead of seeming vague as ghosts, each word was astonishingly prominent....
>
> "We must go," she said, rather surprising Helen by her decision.
>
> (145–6)

So the invitation is accepted.

The picnic on Monte Rosa furthers the plot sequence by being the occasion on which Terence Hewet begins to take a

SYMBOLIC INTRUSIONS IN *THE VOYAGE OUT*

serious interest in Rachel Vinrace. The occasion assumes, at the same time, a symbolic aspect. As Virginia Woolf's art develops, her writing becomes more complex. Here, in her first novel, she is already selecting certain scenes, actions, and events and presenting them in a multi-layered way. In her mature fiction these are more fully integrated into the overall symbolic framework of the novel. This is appropriate in *To the Lighthouse*, for instance, because there she is writing an essentially symbolist work which she calls an 'elegy'. *The Voyage Out*, however, is a traditional novel, so such instances as the following add depth and richness to the kind of story she is telling, which is one that any nineteenth-century novelist might have told before her.

When the little group reaches the summit, exhausted, they are overcome by the magnificence of what they see. In a lyric passage that flows easily in its language, the unfolding scene is described:

> Before them they beheld an immense space – grey sands running into forest, and forest merging in mountains, and mountains washed by air, the infinite distances of South America. A river ran across the plain, as flat as the land, and appearing quite as stationary.

> (153)

As most of these people are by nature inarticulate, they convey the immensity of what they feel by gesture, and Virginia Woolf's description of how they react is tinged with humour: Evelyn Murgatroyd 'took hold of the hand that was next to her; it chanced to be Miss Allan's hand'(153). Their absorption in the spectacle is such that they become unconcerned about each other's personality and act unselfconsciously.

Hewet, on the other hand, who is a novelist and therefore an observer and analyst of human nature who articulates his observations, acts here as a detached observer, summing up the others in the way that Bernard (in a more extended and symbolic way) will sum up the lives of the other characters in *The Waves*. Keeping the surface narrative going, Virginia Woolf explores the scene through Hewet's reflections. He goes on a little in advance of the others and then looks back at them. First, he describes what is literally there, which is a group of

5

VIRGINIA WOOLF AND THE POETRY OF FICTION

windswept people standing silently in a row. But the ordinary language in which this is described has a subtle suggestiveness about it. They are momentarily transfigured in the stillness of their response to the landscape.

> He observed how strangely the people standing in a row with their figures bent slightly forward and their clothes plastered by the wind to the shape of their bodies resembled naked statues.
>
> (153)

Hewet sees that ordinary dull people can take on something of the grandeur that confronts them. By following through the image of the statues he then makes his thoughts explicit.

> On their pedestal of earth they looked unfamiliar and noble, but in another moment they had broken their rank, and he had to see to the laying out of food. Hirst came to his help, and they handed packets of chicken and bread from one to another.
>
> (153)

The change in diction reflects the change in mode of experience, as there is a move from individual transfiguration to involvement in a social ritual. The phrases 'pedestal of earth' and 'the laying out of food' draw attention to themselves, and in so doing suggest ceremonial and ritual. The 'pedestal of earth' has an odd collocation of ideas. The 'pedestal' reinforces the 'statues' image, but the reference to 'earth' suggests something ancient and primal, all of which colours the group with an unusual solemnity.

The picnic episode reveals qualities of sophistication in its writing rare in first novels. The moment of transcendence moves naturally and easily back into the comedy of manners situation as the little group does battle with an invading army of ants.

> The ants were pouring down a glacier of loose earth heaped between the stones of the ruin – large brown ants with polished bodies.... At Hewet's suggestion it was decided to adopt the methods of modern warfare against an invading army. The table-cloth represented the invaded country, and

SYMBOLIC INTRUSIONS IN *THE VOYAGE OUT*

round it they built barricades of baskets, set up the wine
bottles in a rampart, made fortifications of bread and dug
fosses of salt. When an ant got through it was exposed to a
fire of breadcrumbs, until Susan pronounced that that was
cruel, and rewarded those brave spirits with spoil in the
shape of tongue. Playing this game they lost their stiffness....

(155–6)

Taking stock of the little group combating the ants, Hewet
feels suddenly depressed by the mediocrity of most of his
companions. Helen and Rachel, however, seem to him to be
different from the rest. Helen's personality impresses him as
she laughs genuinely and straightforwardly with Miss Allan so
that she stands out 'from the rest like a great stone woman' (157).
The 'stone woman' image, which links back to the 'statues',
suggests qualities of character the others seem only fleetingly
to possess; she is the primal and mythic woman. He is instantly
attracted to Rachel, sensing that they have something in
common. Their encounter is enacted with economy and
simplicity:

His eye fell upon Rachel.... Hewet crawled up to her on his
knees, with a piece of bread in his hand.
"What are you looking at?" he asked.
She was a little startled, but answered directly, "Human
beings."

(157)

The plainness and simplicity of the language matches the
simplicity of the action. All is pared down in terms of language
and action, so that the encounter between Rachel and Terence
is imbued with a quiet poetic intensity and suggestiveness.

The dance is the next event to further Rachel's story. It fits
into the natural sequence of events following on from the
picnic as it is arranged to celebrate the engagement of Susan
Warrington and Arthur Venning (they became engaged at the
picnic), and their relationship is a foil to that developing
between Rachel and Terence Hewet.

At the picnic Terence had been attracted to Rachel, and
Hirst had attached himself to Helen Ambrose. They had
wandered off in those pairings and then come together again

as a group of four. They sat down and, despite knowing very little about each other, they had talked freely about themselves. The four of them form in the course of the novel a closely integrated square of relationships which centre on Rachel. Rachel's is the most elaborately analysed personality within these relationships. Helen, Terence, and Hirst all influence her in some important way and contribute to her development. Helen, as Rachel's older relative, begins as her guardian and becomes her friend. Hirst and Hewet are friends and contemporaries who have travelled out to Santa Marina together.

Like the novelist who is writing *The Voyage Out*, Hewet is writing a novel; like Virginia Woolf he explores personality. He articulates in particular both what he thinks of Rachel and what he feels for her as he explores the nuances of his own experience. Virginia Woolf explores the personalities of them all. Hirst is a rationalist who fails to reach 'the heart of life' himself, but who experiences vicariously what Hewet and Rachel together achieve. Virginia Woolf's analysis of Rachel's search for her true self and her developing relationship with Hewet is far-reaching; so too is her handling of the complementing relationship between Helen and Hirst. As Rachel grows closer to Hewet, Helen feels excluded; and Hirst sees less of his friend who becomes increasingly preoccupied with Rachel. Helen then becomes the friend and confidante of Hirst. The analysis of the platonic friendship between the older woman and the younger man who respond to each other is an innovative theme tied in with the traditional situation of the young lovers. This fluid pattern or square of relationships develops through shifts in emphasis and direction. It is firmly set in motion at the dance.

Rachel and Hirst, however, get off to a bad start. The impossibility of dancing together is followed by an equally unsatisfactory effort at conversation. Because he is ill at ease in the company of an inexperienced young woman (they are actually the same age) he reveals the worst aspects of his personality. He upsets Rachel by being insultingly patronizing, and before long he leaves her, and she escapes into the garden where Hewet finds her. Her fury is channelled into understanding through conversation with the sensitive and humane Hewet who both understands and cares about Hirst, and is anxious at the same time that this young woman shall not have a tainted view of life because of her exposure to the chauvinism of his friend.

Hewet is in many ways the ideal man, the ideal lover. He is intelligent and he is visionary. He is both involved in life and able to detach himself from life in order to understand it. His mind is both creative and analytic. He is the androgynous male. (Evelyn says of him to Rachel: 'I had a long talk with Terence the other night. I felt we really were friends after that. There's something of a woman in him'(302).) Hewet contributes to Rachel's development in terms of thought and articulacy. But apart from his functional role in relation to Rachel, his role *vis-à-vis* the novel as a whole is of major importance. He brings it to a conclusion; his response to the people around him in the hotel after Rachel's death is a kind of summing up. Rachel's changing attitude to him is a measure of her development. His friendship with her reveals that his arrogance and aloofness is more to do with manner than an expression of his true nature. Virginia Woolf probes beneath the surface of Hewet's character to reveal a human being of intellectual integrity who is capable of passion and genuine friendship.

When Hewet has calmed Rachel, and she begins to forget Hirst's insult, they go off together, and feeling much at ease in his company she enters into the spirit of the occasion. Virginia Woolf makes good use here of lesser characters as commentators on the main action of the novel, as when, for instance, Mrs Elliot talks to Mrs Thornbury of Rachel and Hewet:

> "They seem to find a great deal to say to each other," said Mrs. Elliot, looking significantly at the backs of the couple as they turned away. "Did you notice at the picnic? He was the only person who could make her utter."

(185)

Rachel blossoms at the dance:

> She was flushed and looked very happy, and Helen was struck by the fact that in this mood she was certainly more attractive than the generality of young women. She had never noticed it so clearly before.

(191)

VIRGINIA WOOLF AND THE POETRY OF FICTION

After confessing that "She'd no idea that dances could be so delightful", she concludes; "I've changed my view of life completely"(191). At this Helen suggests to Hirst ways in which he could contribute to her education. While Rachel and Hewet have been dancing, Helen and Hirst have been talking and have grown to understand each other much better. Hirst expresses this very strongly:

> "You can't think," he exclaimed, speaking almost with emotion, "what a difference it makes finding some one to talk to! Directly I saw you I felt you might possibly understand me. I'm very fond of Hewet, but he hasn't the remotest idea what I'm like. You're the only woman I've ever met who seems to have the faintest conception of what I mean when I say a thing."
>
> (189)

The dance is such a success that even when the musicians pack up their instruments in the small hours the dancers are reluctant to stop. Rachel improvises at the piano so that they can go on. Now the dance moves into a new phase as steps are invented to fit the music. The movement on the dance floor is spontaneous, free of convention. The unrestrained extravagance of the improvised dancing concludes with the great circular dance which ends with the disarray of people tumbling all over the place. At this stage in the evening there is a hint of carnival and of night revels. They come to an end with the dawn, and with the dawn, too, there is a confrontation with reality. The people who had been completely taken out of themselves as they abandoned themselves to the shifting rhythms of Rachel's playing, suddenly become self-conscious in the dawn light.

When the crowd disperses Rachel plays Bach to herself, and some of the younger people come back into the room to listen to her. The music endows them with a kind of grandeur, as the splendour of nature had influenced the little group standing on the top of Monte Rosa. There the influence was more mystical and general. Here the actual visionary experience is described in a specific way. The music first of all calms and soothes the mind. It then shapes itself into a form that is

SYMBOLIC INTRUSIONS IN *THE VOYAGE OUT*

likened to a particular kind of physical structure: 'as if they saw a building with spaces and columns succeeding each other rising in the empty space'(196). From the shape of the music comes their vision of their own lives, and also a transcendent vision of life itself:

> Then they began to see themselves and their lives, and the whole of human life advancing nobly under the direction of the music.
>
> (196)

As she plays Rachel holds them in thrall and they are ennobled; when she stops they want only to sleep.

In the early dawn light Rachel and Helen accompanied by Hewet and Hirst make their way through the village and up the hill towards the villa. When they reach the turning for the villa the young men are reluctant to depart, so all four sit on the ground together. They are all in harmony with each other, and they sit in silence. Each is quite distinctly enclosed within her or his own separateness. 'Near though they sat, and familiar though they felt, they seemed mere shadows to each other'(198). Here Virginia Woolf makes her point implicity through the image of the 'shadows'. But when the two men leave, walking off together in silence, she makes the same point explicitly:

> they went for a walk, during which they scarcely spoke, and never mentioned the names of the two women, who were, to a considerable extent, the subject of their thoughts. They did not wish to share their impressions. They returned to the hotel in time for breakfast.
>
> (199)

Already in her first novel Virginia Woolf reveals her ability to create scenes and episodes which, in a Jamesian manner, expand from those particular incidents into the whole fabric of the novel at another kind of level. And one such scene is, of course, that of the dance. On the morning after it, Rachel goes off for a walk in order to be alone with her own thoughts. Her head is obviously full of all that had taken place on the previous evening. Virginia Woolf's gloss is significant: 'The night was encroaching upon the day'(204). An interesting aspect of Rachel's walk through the olive grove is that the walk is described authorially because Rachel is unaware, except in the most general terms, of where she is walking: 'She did not see distinctly where she was going, the trees and the landscape appearing only as masses of green and blue, with an occasional space of differently coloured sky'(204). The reason why 'the night was encroaching upon the day' is that Virginia Woolf is converting a literal happening into psychological experience. The whole episode of the night, with its exhilarating and harmonious world of the dance followed first by the soothing mystic experience of Rachel's piano playing and then by the disillusion of the dawn, continues to live after the event itself has passed. For Rachel, as for Hewet and Hirst, something of the experience continues. The night has encroached. The experience of the night is sharpened as it is filtered through Rachel's consciousness where it is recollected in its essence:

> Hewet, Hirst, Mr. Venning, Miss Allan, the music, the light, the dark trees in the garden, the dawn, – as she walked they went surging round in her head, a tumultuous background from which the present moment, with its opportunity for doing exactly as she liked, sprung more wonderfully vivid even than the night before.

(204)

What Virginia Woolf is, in addition, examining here is the nature of time, her theory being that the present is sprung from the past so that we take our past along with us in the present, and then on into the future. Life is a continuum enlarged by significant moments, the effect of which endures and adds up to the whole that we make of our lives.

In her state of heightened consciousness, Rachel then undergoes a mystical experience whereby she learns something very profound about herself. The experience is connected with an object outside herself, a tree. Besides showing Rachel's particular state the incident shows in a more general way the power of the mind to influence the way we perceive things. A distinction is drawn between the ordinary nature of the object and the extraordinary apprehension of it: 'It was an ordinary tree, but to her it appeared so strange that it might have been the only tree in the world'(204–5). After a passage of straightforward narrative, the reader is suddenly confronted

SYMBOLIC INTRUSIONS IN *THE VOYAGE OUT*

by the contrived syntax in which Rachel's exalted experience is expressed. The language is, moreover, suddenly more suggestive, controlled by imagery of light and dark:

> Dark was the trunk in the middle, and the branches sprang here and there, leaving jagged intervals of light between them as distinctly as if it had but that second risen from the ground.
>
> (205)

The description is shot through with energy and menace. The effect of the syntactic inversion at the beginning of the sentence, whereby the monosyllabic word 'Dark' takes the stress, which is then rhythmically reinforced by the monosyllabic word 'trunk' which takes the next stress, is a re-creation of the violence – it is as if one had received a blow – of the experience. Virginia Woolf makes use of the ritual power of language in this way to arrest the flow of her narrative, thereby giving the reader access to a different mode of experience. She then reverts to a plainness of language to describe the subsiding of the experience, but a simple repetition of the phrase 'for a lifetime' at the centre of the statement asserts the enduring nature of that experience:

> Having seen a sight that would last her for a lifetime, and for a lifetime would preserve that second, the tree once more sank into the ordinary ranks of trees, and she was able to seat herself in its shade and to pick the red flowers with the thin green leaves which were growing beneath it.
>
> (205)

Moments such as this assume a mythic quality as they linger in the consciousness, the objects associated with them becoming symbolic. Much later, when Rachel is beset by the bewildering shifts of mood associated with being in love, the moment by the tree is recalled authorially:

> Best of all were the moods when for no reason again this stress of feeling slackened, and life went on as usual, only with a joy and colour in its events that was unknown before; they had a significance like that which she had seen in the tree....
>
> (272)

13

In the calm that follows the experience of transcendence Rachel sits in the shade of the tree and reads a random page of the Gibbon she had received that morning from Hirst. Her perceptions are sharpened because of her experience, so much so that the words she reads seem more vivid.

> They seemed to drive roads back to the very beginning of the world, on either side of which the populations of all times and countries stood in avenues, and by passing down them all knowledge would be hers....
>
> (206)

Rachel's intense experience of the present is further reinforced as she links it back through time to prehistory. From this point on, in the novel, the primitive is increasingly evoked, particularly in the exploration of the nature of human love as the relationship between Rachel and Terence Hewet develops.

What Rachel is looking for in Gibbon is knowledge, but it is knowledge of life that she is really after. The thought of knowledge excites her, but as she shuts her book and walks on she realizes that the real cause of her excitement is her association with the two young men, Hirst and Hewet. She has also a new awareness of what it is to be a woman associating socially for the first time in her life with men of her own age who take her seriously and on her own terms. The momentum of her thought carries her forward energetically, but then, as her mood shifts, she realizes how tired she is and sits down again. She contemplatively allows her mind to become absorbed by a butterfly, 'a great yellow butterfly, which was opening and closing its wings very slowly on a little flat stone'. The thing she observes exactly matches her melancholy frame of mind, as it opens and closes its wings 'very slowly'. It is here at the conclusion of the chapter that she asks herself the momentous question that is at the centre of the novel, and which is at the core of the educational process initiated by Richard Dalloway's kiss, and sponsored by the wise guidance of her aunt, Helen Ambrose: 'What is it to be in love?'(207). It is the essence of Rachel's 'voyage out' into life; that this is so is suggested by Virginia Woolf's reference to the 'unknown sea' which underpins the trite words 'What is it to be in love?' with something of the awesomeness and perplexity that Rachel feels in facing the unknown in life and within human relationships:

> "What is it to be in love?" she demanded, after a long silence; each word as it came into being seemed to shove itself out into an unknown sea.
>
> (207)

The author fuses the inner and the outer experience in her use of imagery: then the butterfly flies off, and Rachel takes a firm hold of her disturbing thought and resolutely returns to the villa, facing the reality of her life.

> Hypnotised by the wings of the butterfly, and awed by the discovery of a terrible possibility in life, she sat for some time longer. When the butterfly flew away, she rose, and with her two books beneath her arm returned home again, much as a soldier prepared for battle.
>
> (207)

The episodes of the picnic and the dance reveal a quality of writing that transforms the overtly traditional structure of the novel into a more searching kind of narrative. In other words, they afford a glimpse of the substructure that constitutes the modern novel and which lurks below and subverts the surface narrative. What is enacted at the surface is the novel of realism. What runs below it is the poetically resonating texture of its symbolic structure.

Chapter Two

'SHAPING FANTASIES' IN
NIGHT AND DAY

The story of *Night and Day* is a simple one. It follows, in broadest outline, the story of young lovers kept apart by misunderstanding, their own search for truth, and the day-to-day happenings of the outside world of family and society. At the end of the novel four young people become engaged to be married, and are all set to live happily ever after in the true fairy-tale manner. This outline belongs to the traditional convention of comedy, whether Shakespearean or in the kind of fictional treatment it is given by Jane Austen. The essential genre of this novel is, therefore, that of comedy in the English literary tradition. Virginia Woolf's handling of the comedy structure is, however, original. It is, in particular, the spirit of that tradition that she exploits, but she also enriches it with her own individuality. She does this largely by underwriting the prose of the surface story and plot complication with the 'poetry of existence'; this poetry has to do with the quality of existence, with a visionary dimension that is shot through the mundane.

The innovative writing underpinning this very traditional novel is of a kind that has parallels in *The Voyage Out*, one of the most obvious being the use Virginia Woolf makes of the guardian figure. In the 'tragedy' of *The Voyage Out* Helen Ambrose is a figure of fate embroidering the destiny of the doomed Rachel. Her cast of mind is pessimistic; she has from the outset presentiments of impending doom. In the 'comedy' of *Night and Day*, on the other hand, the guardian figure, Mrs Hilbery, is a kind of fairy godmother. She is also cast in the role of the wise fool. Hints of this role are placed imperceptibly in the novel from its earliest stages, but as the

'SHAPING FANTASIES' IN *NIGHT AND DAY*

novel gains momentum in its second half the guardian role of Mrs Hilbery is made more explicit.

Mrs Hilbery is a Mrs Wilcox-like visionary figure. She lives in the vague poetic dream world of her own imagination, and she is obsessed by Shakespeare who nourishes her imaginative life. She is a delightful hostess provided someone else attends to the practical details of bread and butter. She is imbued with the spirit of poetry whereas her husband, like so many of Virginia Woolf's other father figures (Ridley Ambrose, Mr Ramsay) is a rational man, a man of fact, a scholar. She is herself an embodiment of the values of the past in a rapidly changing world.

> In times gone by, Mrs. Hilbery had known all the poets, all the novelists, all the beautiful women and distinguished men of her time. These being now either dead or secluded in their infirm glory, she made her house a meeting-place for her own relations, to whom she would lament the passing of the great days of the nineteenth century ....
>
> (31–2)

Her house is dedicated to keeping alive the memory of her visionary father, the Victorian poet Richard Alardyce. Through him, and her mother who is his devotee, Katharine takes on his visionary capacity and through it the wisdom that is handed down from the past. His shrine is the symbolic centre of the house. At the surface comedy level visitors are shown his 'relics' preserved in a chapel-like room. As well as the received wisdom that comes to her through her mother, Katharine undergoes a mystical experience in front of her grandfather's portrait when she realizes that in the picture he is the same age that she now is. She comes to know him for herself, and places before him her own life with its perplexities, much as one would make an offering to a deity: 'and instead of laying her withered flowers upon his shrine, she brought him her own perplexities – perhaps a gift of greater value, should the dead be conscious of gifts, than flowers and incense and adoration' (338).

Ralph keeps vigil at the house as at a shrine because it contains the object of his adoration, Katharine, but he is also partly in love with the house because of the vision enshrined in it. It seems in different ways to be a place of light and security from which he is temporarily excluded:

> Lights burnt in the three long windows of the drawing-room. The space of the room behind became, in Ralph's vision, the centre of the dark, flying wilderness of the world.... In this little sanctuary were gathered together several different people, but their identity was dissolved in the general glory of something that might, perhaps, be called civilization....
>
> (418)

Although Mrs Hilbery dislikes much in the present age, particularly its changing values and attitudes, she does not herself criticize the young people she comes in contact with. Instead she offers them her own genuine warmth and her vision, and her house is a meeting-place for them:

> She welcomed them very heartily to her house, told them her stories, gave them sovereigns and ices and good advice, and weaved round them romances which had generally no likeness to the truth.
>
> (32)

This kind of writing is deceptively simple. Mrs Hilbery seems to be mocked by the author for her indulgence and her illusions. Yet contained in the above sentence are the three elements which, as the novel progresses, make Mrs Hilbery the kind guardian of the young people of her family and their friends; her wisdom lies not too far below the surface of her apparent folly. The three elements that characterize her role are affection, wisdom, and an ability to negotiate the truth by apparently wrapping it up in fantasy and romance. She gives to the young who come under her influence what they most want to have, she offers them good advice, and she learns the truth about them by weaving her romance round them.

Ralph and Katharine, like Mrs Hilbery, both weave romance and tell stories (they also try to deny their validity) in the course of their journey towards the reconciliation of their respective dreams with reality. His final test of Katharine and the validity of his dream of her had been to take her to visit his family. She passes the test with flying colours, and he

'SHAPING FANTASIES' IN *NIGHT AND DAY*

explains his action to her: 'I've done my best to see you as you are, without any of this damned romantic nonsense' (404). But she rejects what she still considers to be his dream of her and blames him for doing exactly what her mother does:

> "You come and see me among flowers and pictures, and think me mysterious, romantic, and all the rest of it. Being yourself very inexperienced and very emotional, you go home and invent a story about me, and now you can't separate me from the person you've imagined me to be. You call that, I suppose, being in love; as a matter of fact it's being in delusion. All romantic people are the same," she added. "My mother spends her life in making stories about the people she's fond of. But I won't have you do it about me, if I can help it."
>
> (404)

In the event she can't help it. And what is more she has her own habitual romance which contains her idealized version of him: 'the forest, the ocean beach, the leafy solitudes, the magnanimous hero' (284). Ultimately Katharine is compelled to acknowledge the truth of the romance her mother weaves for her. Like an ancient seer her mother 'croons' her tale. She is trying to convince her that her feelings for Ralph prove her to be in love with him. To do this she tells her own love story by first recalling herself and her husband as 'fantastically attired, clasping hands upon a moonlit beach, with roses swinging in the dusk'. She then enlarges on that image of her youth.

> "We were in a little boat going out to a ship at night," she began. "The sun had set and the moon was rising over our heads. There were lovely silver lights upon the waves...."
>
> (511)

As the story reaches the mind of the listener it becomes further transformed. It becomes the archetypal story of all youth ('the ancient fairy-tale') and then Katharine's own imagination takes over:

> The ancient fairy-tale fell roundly and harmoniously upon Katharine's ears. Yes, there was the enormous space of the

19

VIRGINIA WOOLF AND THE POETRY OF FICTION

sea; there were the three green lights upon the steamer; the cloaked figures climbed up on deck....

(512)

Her mother weaves her romance, she gives her advice – 'We must have faith in our vision' – and she will enable her to be possessed of what she most wants to have. No wonder Katharine looks upon her as if 'she were some magician'(513). The effect of Mrs Hilbery's soft crooning words is 'a riveting together of the shattered fragments of the world'(512): she does that for Katharine here at the level of vision; and Katharine finds her 'equally wise and equally benignant'(510). She will later, like a magician, take practical steps to create the right situation for the fulfilling of that vision. In the course of the novel Katharine learns how to unify the romance of her vision and the mundane existence of the 'real' world, the 'night' and the 'day'; in a tranquil moment she looks upon Ralph and sees his action as an emblem of the unity she seeks: as he discusses tides and ships with an old boatman she observes his 'strangeness, his romance, his power to leave her side and take part in the affairs of men...'(486).

Mrs Hilbery's guardianship role has two aspects to it, that of the visionary or seer, and that of the magician. The former aspect is reflected in the penetrating quality of her eyes. Her way of procedure is to spin a web of words, usually fanciful or irrelevant, while at the same time her eyes search out the nugget of truth she is after. Ralph becomes aware of her ability when her gaze is turned on him:

During this speech... Ralph felt that Mrs. Hilbery was talking to him apart, with a desire to ascertain something about him which she veiled purposely by the vagueness of her words. He felt curiously encouraged and heartened by the beam in her eye rather than by her actual words. From the distance of her age and sex she seemed to be waving to him, hailing him as a ship sinking beneath the horizon might wave its flag of greeting to another setting out upon the same voyage. He bent his head, saying nothing, but with a curious certainty that she had read an answer to her inquiry that satisfied her.

(451–2)

'SHAPING FANTASIES' IN *NIGHT AND DAY*

And when she turns up in his office (after she has come back from Stratford in order to fetch him back to Katharine), he senses again through her vague discourse that she 'possesses all the facts of their situation'. No words of explanation are required.

With a slight variation on her manner of procedure, she allows her daughter Katharine to talk at length about Ralph and his family while she appears to listen, adding only the odd comment. She in fact hears very little, but she learns what she wants to know by observing her daughter closely as she speaks:

> Mrs. Hilbery listened without making any remark for a considerable time. She seemed to draw her conclusions rather by looking at her daughter than by listening to her, and, if cross-examined she would probably have given a highly inaccurate version of Ralph Denham's life-history except that he was penniless, fatherless, and lived at Highgate – all of which was much in his favour.
>
> (510)

In her 'magician' aspect she fulfils a *deus ex machina* function in the novel. Unobtrusively, at first, she seems to appear on the scene at a moment of confusion or crisis in order to set things right, as when, for instance, she turns up at the grocer's shop in Lincoln. Ralph is contemplating a marriage without romance or true vision, but she points him in the right direction (i.e. by leading him off to her daughter) – though at the surface level of the narrative she is merely getting his help in order to find Katharine, William, and the ruins they have gone off to explore. As the novel draws to its conclusion, however, the magician/fairy godmother nature of her activity becomes more obvious and explicit. Katharine, greatly relieved when her mother helps her to understand the nature of her feelings, actually refers to her 'as if, indeed, she were some magician'(513). Then with a complete change in mode of writing to that of fantasy or fairy tale, Virginia Woolf blurs the various roles of mother, magician, and fairy godmother into one as Katharine changes from being an independent young woman of twenty-seven into a little child.

21

VIRGINIA WOOLF AND THE POETRY OF FICTION

Once more she felt that instead of being a grown woman, used to advise and command, she was only a foot or two raised above the long grass and the little flowers and entirely dependent upon the figure of indefinite size whose head went up into the sky, whose hand was in hers, for guidance....

Mrs. Hilbery nodded her head in a manner which indicated complete understanding, and the immediate conception of certain plans for the future. She swept up her flowers, breathed in their sweetness, and, humming a little song about a miller's daughter, left the room.

(513–14)

Virginia Woolf gives shape to Mrs Hilbery's role of guardian of the young in a playful manner by increasingly drawing on the genre of Shakespearean comedy, and by herself spinning an increasingly complicated web of fantasy and romance round both the young lovers and the older guardian figure. The Shakespearean aspect of Mrs Hilbery's activity and attitude grows naturally out of her lifelong dedication to and obsession with Shakespeare. It is given full rein in the spring when she goes on a pilgrimage to Shakespeare's tomb in Stratford. In her absence the muddle of the young people's lives becomes increasingly alarming, and it is suggested that she alone is capable of sorting out the confusion. Her husband, refusing like Jane Austen's Mr Bennet to take responsibility for the actions and behaviour of the young members of his family, summons his wife to return from Stratford which she does. Then in a fairy godmother fashion she gets into a carriage, collects Ralph from Lincoln's Inn Fields, and William from Whitehall (chance brings Cassandra back) and assembles them together at her house, where they are finally and formally sorted out into in their true pairings: 'Jack shall have Jill;/ Nought shall go ill.'

In moments of awareness and also in those moments in which the relation between dream and reality is being tested out in the novels the presence of the moon is often indicated. At this level of the novel's narration there is a shift to a poetic mode of writing which at times creates an atmosphere similar to that of Shakespearean comedy. The pervasive presence of

'SHAPING FANTASIES' IN *NIGHT AND DAY*

the moon especially evokes the world of Shakespearean comedy in general and of *A Midsummer Night's Dream* in particular. By spring (the action begins in autumn) the protagonists of the love story all at one time or another think they are mad, so that love is linked with madness, and the spirit of poetry pervades their reflections, all of which has obvious parallels with *A Midsummer Night's Dream*. Where interpretation of Virginia Woolf's fiction in terms of either its mythic content or use of allusion becomes questionable it is usually when suggestive hints within a text are picked up and used for absolute interpretation, regardless either of other balancing elements or of more significant features. Having said that, however, allusions, both explicit and veiled, to Shakespearean comedy are so abundant in this work that their presence compels attention.

An overt Shakespearean celebration of moonlight in association with love opens Act V of *The Merchant of Venice*. Lorenzo and Jessica, by virtue of their love for each other, join company with the great lovers of the past. Every speech of their dialogue opens with reference to the quality of the night ('In such a night'):

> *Lor.* The moon shines bright: in such a night as this,
> When the sweet wind did gently kiss the trees
> And they did make no noise, in such a night
> Troilus methinks mounted the Troyan walls....
>
> (II.1–4)

Their exchange leads to a declaration of love. In *A Midsummer Night's Dream*, however, the presence of the moon controls the whole action of the play from the slowly waning moon of its opening to the new moon four days later when nuptials are celebrated. At the outset Hippolyta encourages Theseus by saying that 'Four nights will quickly dream away the time'. There is in Shakespeare's play a fascinating exploration of dream/vision, and Duke Theseus' great speech on the nature of imagination contains comments that are appropriate to *Night and Day*, which Virginia Woolf first thought of calling *Dreams and Realities*, which in its central theme links love with poetry and the imaginative life, and in which the young lovers temporarily forsake the world of 'cool reason'.

VIRGINIA WOOLF AND THE POETRY OF FICTION

> Lovers and madmen have such seething brains,
> Such shaping fantasies, that apprehend
> More than cool reason ever comprehends.
> The lunatic, the lover, and the poet,
> Are of imagination all compact....

and Hippolyta's answer, moreover, makes fair comment on the conclusion of the novel.

> But all the story of the night told over,
> And all their minds transfigured so together,
> More witnesseth than fancy's images,
> And grows to something of great constancy,
> But, howsoever, strange and admirable.

Reference to the moon is introduced early in the novel. Before people arrive for the fortnightly meeting in Mary Datchet's room, Mary enjoys the quietness of her room and reflects on this in a comparison which takes her beyond the world of her room:

> Mary was led to think of the heights of a Sussex down, and the swelling green circle of some camp of ancient warriors. The moonlight would be falling there so peacefully now, and she could fancy the rough pathway of silver upon the wrinkled skin of the sea.
>
> (43)

The primitive scene evoked, bearing additional suggestions of moonlight and fairy rings, is a correlative to Mary's state of mind. For six months her friendship with Ralph has blossomed.

A little later, after William Rodney has read his paper on the Elizabethan use of metaphor, and when conversation gets under way, Katharine, who is talking to Mary, draws back the curtain and looks purposefully at the moon:

> Mary then saw Katharine raise her eyes again to the moon, with a contemplative look in them, as though she were setting that moon against the moon of other nights, held in memory.
>
> (56)

The wording is significant. Katharine is drawing on the past, and her past is largely literary in association (Shakespearean

'SHAPING FANTASIES' IN *NIGHT AND DAY*

in particular). The modern world of Mary Datchet, of working for the suffrage movement and of the kind of literary meeting she has just attended, will enable her 'to join the present to the past'. But an unexpressed reason for Katharine's enjoyment of the meeting is that she comes up against Ralph Denham again. His intelligent though abrasive personality intrigues her. When the gathering disperses there follows one of those evening walks in which Virginia Woolf allows the poetic and visionary layer of the novel to obtrude.

Ralph follows Katharine and William Rodney as they make their way through the London streets to the Embankment. He keeps a safe distance from them so that he remains unobserved. The narrative comment with its reference to the quality of the night and the moonlight signals a narrative shift to the visionary level of experience:

> The night was very still, and on such nights [cf.
> Shakespeare's 'In such a night...'], when the traffic thins
> away, the walker becomes conscious of the moon in the
> street, as if the curtains of the sky had been drawn apart,
> and the heaven lay bare, as it does in the country.
>
> (60)

Ralph Denham seems to be wandering in a dream, some strange force appearing to have taken control of his actions:

> Denham had no conscious intention of following
> Katharine....
>
> Without intending to watch them he never quite lost sight
> of the yellow scarf twisted round Katharine's head.
>
> Denham had no feeling of irritation with Katharine, but
> rather a half-dreamy acquiescence in the course of the
> world.
>
> Denham kept, if that is the right expression for an
> involuntary action, one filament of his mind upon them.
>
> (60–1)

When William and Katharine reach the river he bids her look at the moon on the water. In his halting caricature of a

25

VIRGINIA WOOLF AND THE POETRY OF FICTION

proposal he asks her to look at 'the iridescence round the moon' and claims to be 'half a poet', and continues: 'If I could write – ah, that would be another matter. I shouldn't bother you to marry me then, Katharine'(62). Their exchange continues in this kind of unsatisfactory way, but he realizes from Katharine's reactions that he has appeared foolish: after they separate he goes off muttering to himself 'Heaven forbid that I should ever make a fool of myself again'. Within this brief incident, then, there is an interplay of lunatic, lover, and poet in a humorous manner as the author berates William for his conventionality and ineptitude.

At the same time, however, she reveals a strand of strong feeling asserting itself below the surface of the fumbling conversation on the Embankment. Katharine asks William if he would recommend marriage for her, and as she does this she keeps her eyes fixed on the moon. After he has elaborated on his affirmative answer and they begin to walk along the Embankment he quotes (actually adapting Sidney) a poem which, in its image of the moon, reflects his own melancholy feelings:

> With how sad steps she climbs the sky,
> How silently and with how wan a face.
>
> (63)

It is obvious that the dreamer, Ralph Denham, has already a stronger hold on Katharine's interest than the man she will soon agree to marry. The situation is skilfully handled. Ralph looks on at the two people he imagines to be in love with each other, whereas one of them, the woman he is himself infatuated with, already but unconsciously returns his feelings. The comedy aspect of the novel, in the *Midsummer Night's Dream* sense, of the confusion of the young lovers is set in motion. At a deeper level, however, it is underpinned by the serious exploration of the nature of love through the complex interplay of dream and reality, more especially in Ralph's and Katharine's search for truth and fulfilment. The elaborate invocation of the moon has signalled their entry into and exploration of their respective dream worlds. The irony of their situation is handled with sensitivity; Virginia Woolf, however, follows this by the comic irony of having William and Ralph go off together after Katharine has taken her cab home.

'SHAPING FANTASIES' IN *NIGHT AND DAY*

Ralph's next encounter with Katharine is in Mary's office. Here the author is creating a situation that parallels the scene on the Embankment, only positions are reversed: Katharine is here an outsider and she imagines that Mary and Ralph have reached an understanding. Later that same night Ralph will encounter his 'phantom woman' in the solitude of his attic room, and Katharine will in a similar way in her room summon up her dream of her ideal hero, and of the nature of true love:

> Not having experience of it herself, her mind had unconsciously occupied itself for some years in dressing up an image of love, and the marriage that was the outcome of love, and the man who inspired love, which naturally dwarfed any examples that came her way. Easily, and without correction by reason, her imagination made pictures, superb backgrounds casting a rich though phantom light upon the facts in the foreground.... The man, too, was some magnanimous hero, riding a great horse by the shore of the sea. They rode through forests together, they galloped by the rim of the sea. But waking, she was able to contemplate a perfectly loveless marriage, as the thing one did actually in real life, for possibly the people who dream thus are those who do the most prosaic things.
>
> (107–8)

Katharine like Ralph, slips in and out of the dream world of her own imagining, but like Ralph, also, she is in control of her life because she is able to distinguish between, and hold in balance, that visionary world of dream (Night) and the 'cool reason' world of reality (Day).

The central confusion that builds up with increasing momentum in the novel is registered by the extent to which the balance between the two worlds breaks down: reality, it seems, has to become submerged in the dream world before it can be fully acknowledged and possessed.

One of the saddest incidents in the book is the one in which Katharine goes to tea in William's rooms; the world of dream and the world of reality are kept rigidly separate, and are seen for what they are. Clearsightedly she sees what her life would amount to if she were to marry William. So bored is she in his company that she drifts into her dream world. Her vision is

VIRGINIA WOOLF AND THE POETRY OF FICTION

one of complete human fulfilment, and Virginia Woolf analyses it as one in which she has found 'the realities of the appearances that dwell in our world'.

> It was a place where feelings were liberated from the constraint which the real world puts upon them; and the process of awakenment was always marked by resignation and a kind of stoical acceptance of facts.

(145)

At this point in the novel Katharine believes that her vision has no validity in the real world, and so she tells William that she is prepared to marry him.

There is a significant difference between the dream worlds of Katharine and Ralph. Ralph, in his visions, always finds a 'real' person (Katharine) though she is enlarged and embellished by his imagination. His dream is, in other words, one of wish-fulfilment, but it remains within the realms of the credible and the possible. He is constantly adjusting the balance between the two worlds of dreams and realities. Katharine's dream is more theoretical and escapist: her vision contains no image of any person known to her in the real world. She seeks there, in other words, what she has been unable to find in the real world. The ideal of her dream is the antithesis of the real man she has just agreed to marry. Yet paradoxically, she is, in seeking her ideal lover, being truer to life than she is in accepting marriage to William Rodney. She will eventually come to recognize the 'magnanimous hero' in Ralph, and her final acceptance of him reduces the gap between the dream and the reality.

When Ralph next visits the Hilbery house he learns of Katharine's engagement to William. He arrives lightheartedly with the realization that only Katharine can fulfil his dreams. When he sees her his dream is brought to life before his eyes, only she is 'more beautiful and strange than his dream of her.... She overflowed the edges of the dream'(150). But the dream is at once shattered when he learns that she is not free. The shattering of his dream is reflected in the way he sees the world around him after he has left the house: 'He made no pattern out of the sights he saw'(161–2). The climate, too – it is winter, and there is a chilly fog – reflects his state of mind.

28

'SHAPING FANTASIES' IN *NIGHT AND DAY*

He sits on a bench and reflects on his position. The 'lowest pitch of his despair' is the realization that his dreams had meant nothing to Katharine (163). In the extreme of his despondency he leaves dreaming and turns to reasoning about his dreams. His view of life is as bleak as his physical position of sitting on a bench on the Embankment in the winter's fog. When Mary meets him in the street one lunchtime shortly before Christmas she is shocked by his altered appearance, and she tells him that he looks as if he were walking in his sleep. Realizing that he is profoundly unhappy, but not knowing why, she invites him to spend Christmas with her family, and he accepts. Virginia Woolf describes her response to him in language that briefly draws her into the fairy-tale aspect of the novel's substructure: 'the mystery of his nature laid more of a spell upon her than she liked'(169). Although she is strong and independent she is nevertheless vulnerable: 'She could not prevent herself from doing now what she had often blamed others of her sex for doing – from endowing her friend with a kind of heavenly fire, and passing her life before it for his sanction'(169).

The bleakest phase of the young lovers' fortunes occurs in winter. By a coincidence the protagonists are all removed to Lincolnshire, Ralph staying with Mary's family, and Katharine and William visiting Katharine's cousins the Otways, only a few miles away. They all, however, take their dreams with them. Looking out of the train window on his way there Ralph sees the landscape as the landscape that Katharine has looked upon. He has, however, put a curb on his dream: 'Since the day when he had heard from Katharine's lips of her engagement, he had refrained from investing his dream of her with the details of real life'(192). He uses his dream now as a conscious escape from reality: it no longer holds for him at its centre the reality that had seemed to be within his grasp. So it is that the late afternoon light on the fields becomes a symbol of Katharine and not the embodiment of her. Yet when he sees Mary on the platform, something in his dream of the ideal woman spills over into the way in which he sees her: 'About her seemed to hang the mist of the winter hedges, and the clear red of the bramble leaves'(192).

Images of Mary and Katharine blur into each other in

VIRGINIA WOOLF AND THE POETRY OF FICTION

Ralph's mind during his stay in Lincolnshire. On the evening of his arrival he watches Mary affectionately stroking her brother's hair and suddenly wishes she were doing that to him. But then, looking at Mary, he seems to see Katharine Hilbery. On his walk into Lincoln with Mary he reflects to himself that it is six weeks since he sat on the Embankment 'watching his visions dissolve in mist' (233). Yet in the course of the walk he is overcome by a sense of Katharine's presence just as he is reflecting on Mary's very considerable human qualities:

> He lost his sense of all that surrounded him; all substantial things – the hour of the day... all this slipped from him. So he might have felt if the earth had dropped from his feet... and the air had been steeped in the presence of one woman.

(235)

Then as they sit at lunch in a comfortable inn it is as if he sees his dream enacted before him: looking out of the window he sees Katharine in the street, and then she disappears. It had suddenly come to him in a flash that Mary loved him; now Mary in a blinding revelation of truth sees that he is in love with Katharine Hilbery. The surface comedy tone is restored when Mrs Hilbery appears on the scene and they all go off together to join the rest of her party. But then the confusion intensifies when Ralph tells Katharine that he is thinking of buying a cottage nearby: she presumes that he is engaged to Mary.

As the confusion grows, elements of fairy tale and romance enter the narrative, and the confusion of the young lovers is expressed with increasing reference to elemental causes of confusion such as mists, fogs, and tempests, all of which have obvious Shakespearean connections.

Tension builds up between William and Katharine on their way back to the house. He is angry with her for the way she has been treating him: 'No one enjoys being made a fool of before other people' (250), and he goes on to catalogue his grievances. She is shocked at the contrast between the strength of his feeling for her and her indifference to him. It moves her to the crisis of breaking off her engagement, which marks a stage

'SHAPING FANTASIES' IN *NIGHT AND DAY*

in her journey to self-knowledge. She had accepted him, she explains, when she was 'in a misty state of mind'(254). She had done so in order to reconcile herself to the world of facts: 'She could only recall a moment, as of waking from a dream, which now seemed to her a moment of surrender'(254). She tries to comfort him.

> The idea came to her that they were like the children in the
> fairy tale who were lost in a wood, and with this in her mind
> she noticed the scattering of dead leaves all round them
> which had been blown by the wind into heaps, a foot or two
> deep, here and there.
>
> (256)

As she fumbles for the right word to explain her true feeling 'she looked vaguely towards the horizon sunk under mist'(257). The nature of her feelings is then imaged in her disorderly appearance: she is sitting on the ground among dead leaves, some of which are attached to her dress, a strand of her hair has come undone and she wears a look of total abstraction. 'She sat there, seeming unconscious of everything'(259). Then, having made it clear that she does not love William, she agrees to marry him. In her dishevelled appearance, her momentary relinquishing of the restraints of behaviour, she has entered more deeply into the dream world, the world suggestive of Shakespeare's young lovers when they are in the wood.

In the meantime the other pair, Ralph and Mary, undergo a parallel situation of confusion and confrontation on the way back to their house. Ralph is struggling not to succumb to the dream which has been renewed by seeing Katharine again.

> He was determined that the glow, the romance, the
> atmosphere of this meeting should not paint what he must
> in future regard as sober facts.
>
> (260)

In a muted tone of voice, similar to that used by Katharine when she said she would marry William, Ralph asks Mary to marry him. She refuses him. What distresses her most is his 'cruellest treachery' in proposing to her when he loves someone else. Later that evening he tries to justify his action by abrogating the power of romantic love:

31

VIRGINIA WOOLF AND THE POETRY OF FICTION

'It's only a story one makes up in one's mind about another person, and one knows all the time it isn't true.... It's a pleasant illusion, but if you're thinking of the risks of marriage, it seems to me that the risk of marrying a person you're in love with is something colossal.'

(265)

Anger and despair become increasingly part of Ralph's confusion. He finds the world to be without order, and he blames Mary for being part of the 'insanely jumbled muddle of a world'(266).

Ralph finds his deepest distress when he turns from his specific personal problem to its more general and universal implications:

it seemed to him that he had been defeated, not so much by Mary as by life itself. He felt himself thrown back to the beginning of life again, where everything has yet to be won; but in extreme youth one has an ignorant hope. He was no longer certain that he would triumph.

(267)

The emotional vacuum of his life leads him to take up a position that comes close to ontological despair.

From this point in the novel Mary is less centrally involved in the 'confusion of the young lovers' plot. She takes her own independent way, choosing work as an antidote to her pain, though she understands the limitations of her choice:

With a brain working and a body working one could keep step with the crowd and never be found out for the hollow machine, lacking the essential thing, that one was conscious of being.

(272)

She adjusts her vision, and exchanges her role of young lover for that of sisterly confidante and friend.

Another character is brought in to take her place as the fourth member in the square of muddled relationships. It is Cassandra, Katharine's cousin whom William met and became infatuated with at Christmas. So the confusion takes a new turn, and puts on a new aspect. In her new role Mary tells Katharine that Ralph is in love with her, and also the truth of

'SHAPING FANTASIES' IN *NIGHT AND DAY*

her own (unreturned) feelings for Ralph. Katharine then visits William and learns that he is falling in love with Cassandra. Their discussion turns on the nature of romance, and Katharine makes an interesting avowal which confirms her inner resemblance to her mother. In attempting to explain to William its significance for her, she has a further glimpse of the reality of her life: it has so far offered her little scope for romance, which she tries to define:

> It was a desire, an echo, a sound; she could drape it in
> colour, see it in form, hear it in music, but not in words; no,
> never in words. She sighed, teased by desires so incoherent,
> so incommunicative.

> (303)

But then, as if unconsciously clearing her way for the achieving of her personal 'romance', she gently frees William to enter his different kind of romance with Cassandra.

Confusion, mental and emotional, which at times is linked imagistically with magic or the fairy world, runs through the novel; it reaches its heights in the concluding chapters. At first there are only muted hints. Often they are connected with atmospheric images such as mist or fog, and characters become fools and madmen. Katharine, for instance, when she understands herself better, looks back to the scene on the heath in Lincolnshire when she let William see that she did not love him, and reflects that 'She had accepted him in a misty state of mind when nothing had its right shape or size'(254). She brings the scene back into her mind so that she can revisit it in the present, and so learn from it:

> So in broad daylight one might revisit the place where one
> has groped and turned and succumbed in utter
> bewilderment in a fog.

> (294)

William refers to his confused state as one of madness. After he admits to Katharine that he loves Cassandra he feels that unless he can see Katharine alone (Ralph has just come into the room) he can never know 'what he had said in a moment of madness, which was not altogether mad, or was it mad?' But

33

VIRGINIA WOOLF AND THE POETRY OF FICTION

he is prevented from seeing her alone by Ralph who takes her off to the river where he makes his eloquent declaration of love – 'I see you everywhere, in the stars, in the river, to me you're everything that exists...'(313) – and then with obvious self-contradiction tells her that he is not in love with her. William refers to the night on which he told Katharine that he loved Cassandra as 'a night of madness'(335).

It is often when the confusion is at its greatest that elements of madness or folly are attached to states of mind. The 'night of madness', reaching its greatest intensity, finds both Ralph and Katharine, on different occasions, wandering in a distraught manner through the London streets at night. The build-up to Ralph's night wandering begins after he has taken Katharine to visit his family. After she leaves and he is alone, the author gives an account of his passionate longing that seems deliberately to reflect the love-sick Orsino's opening speech in Shakespeare's *Twelfth Night*:

> Like a strain of music, the effect of Katharine's presence slowly died from the room in which Ralph sat alone. The music had ceased in the rapture of its melody. He strained to catch the faintest lingering echoes; for a moment the memory lulled him into peace; but soon it failed, and he paced the room so hungry for the sound to come again that he was conscious of no other desire left in life.
>
> (407)

He then goes off to tell Mary Datchet that he is in love with Katharine. On his way there he refers to his love as 'madness, romance, hallucination'(409). Next he sets out on his nightmare journey through the windy streets: the turmoil in his mind is reflected in the turmoil of the night. But authorial comment establishes that 'the whirl of the atmosphere alone was in Denham's mood'(416). He wanders through a windswept world that evokes Dante's circle of lost lovers in the *Inferno*. He sits on a bench and listens to a down-and-out's 'ancient story of disaster and despair'; the story rushes past him in the wind. The storm takes on an increasing imaginative force for Ralph as he builds up a dream of his mental turmoil:

'SHAPING FANTASIES' IN *NIGHT AND DAY*

an odd image came to his mind of a lighthouse besieged by
the flying bodies of lost birds, who were dashed senselessly
by the gale, against the glass....

(417–18)

The image of the lighthouse and the lost birds from the
dream persists, and he takes the logical step of walking towards
a 'house of light', the beneficent house of the Hilberys, which
becomes merged in his heightened mental state with the image
of the lighthouse from his dream. Standing in front of the
house, dream and reality merge as he confronts the 'shrine'
which houses the object of his search, Katharine Hilbery. The
description of the house has the charged and condensed
quality of pure poetry as he mentally journeys through the
house until he reaches Katharine and apprehends the reality
of her existence as 'a shape of light'.

In weaving together the different images the passage as a
whole modulates into a return to the original cluster of images
of the storm (lighthouse, lost birds) but with positions altered
so that Ralph considers himself actually to be one of the 'lost
birds'. Here Virginia Woolf has used the literal structure of
the dream sequence. Ralph, to begin with, had been outside,
looking on at the flying bodies of birds and at the lighthouse.
Then he became 'both lighthouse and bird'. Finally, he is
simply exhausted like one of the lost birds. An image had
been brought to life, and he had been caught up in its life.
The intensity of experience is deflated as William Rodney comes
out of the house and the two men walk off together. Their confusion and misery forms a bond between them, but Rodney
calls it folly:

'My God, Denham, what fools we both are!' Rodney
exclaimed. They looked at each other queerly in the light of
the lamp. Fools! They seemed to confess to each other the
extreme depths of their folly.

(423)

Katharine's nightmare journey is of a different nature. She
literally sets out through the streets looking for Ralph, with a
sense of her urgent need for him 'as if she were waking from
some dream'. What she feels is 'blankness and desolation' (468).

Her confusion clarifies itself into the form of desire, a desire that is 'wild, irrational, unexplained, resembling something felt in childhood'. She wanders until she is mentally and physically exhausted, and then goes to Mary Datchet's flat to see if he is there. By that time her state has become irrational. She becomes so fixed in her panic that she has to be rescued by Mary's common sense and eventually taken by her to Cheyne Walk where Ralph is waiting for her.

Cassandra enters into the plot at the point at which the fairy-tale or romance elements become more insistent. Her journey to London is a voyage into a romantic world of magic and enchantment: the train takes her 'straight to the centre of her most romantic world'(361). As she goes in to dinner on her first evening the scene before her is 'one of magical brilliancy'. Later in the evening when she is alone with Katharine she notes her melancholy, and Katharine says cryptically to her:

'Ah, but it's only ten o'clock....
'At twelve my horses turn into rats and off I go. The illusion fades. But I accept my fate. I make hay while the sun shines.'

(374–5)

and she goes off to see Mary Datchet.

Love, magic, confusion, and madness all become increasingly bound up together as the novel draws to its conclusion, although after the two night wanderings the tone lightens. Cassandra notes of Katharine, for instance, that she has grown absent-minded: she forgets to serve the pudding at lunch, or holds out a cup into which she has omitted to pour tea. And she will leave the house with a piece of bread and butter in her hand. And more generally, Cassandra has found, 'Every one seems to me a little queer'(384). Mr Hilbery thinks that all the talk about Shakespeare 'had acted as a soporific, or rather as an incantation upon Katharine'(529). On the night on which he had been unable to elicit any rational explanation from her for what had occurred, he drew the conclusion that 'Civilization had been very profoundly and unpleasantly overthrown that evening'(505). When Mrs Hilbery has sorted out all the muddles and got the young lovers together in their

'SHAPING FANTASIES' IN *NIGHT AND DAY*

right relationships she sings 'her strange, half-earthly song of dawns and sunsets, of great poets, and the unchanged spirit of noble loving which they had taught, so that nothing changes, and one age is linked with another, and no one dies, and we all meet in spirit, until she appeared oblivious of any one in the room' (526). By the final chapter civilization is restored, Mr Hilbery presides over a feast (531) and music is played. Katharine and Ralph walk out into the moonlight and she 'held in her hands for one brief moment the globe which we spend our lives in trying to shape, round, whole, and entire without the confusion of chaos'. As they make their way to the river, and she feels his arm stiffen, she knows that 'they had entered the enchanted region' (537).

It has taken Mrs Hilbery's intervention to bring chaos to order. With her help Ralph and Katharine reach a position of trust in, and acceptance of, the power of visionary love. But she is only the guardian of their struggle to reach their unifying vision of life. They have had to make their own way in order to turn their dream into actuality, her help bringing their quest to its conclusion. Their journey has been an exploration of the validity of vision, conducted, as we have seen, through an investigation of the relationship between dream and reality. Both Ralph and Katharine lost their sense of perspective; they had been so taken over by their respective dreams that they had temporarily relinquished their grasp of reality. Their experience of pain, anguish, and incomprehension, which is expressed in the confusion of the night wanderings, is very like that of Shakespeare's young lovers in *A Midsummer Night's Dream*, although errors that are externally generated in the play are internally generated in the novel. In both the play and the novel it requires an external agent to bring the dream world to order again. The mood and spirit of the novel with its constant references to enchantments, dreams, magic, fairy tale, confusions, fogs and mists, its evocations of the moon, and in particular its insistence on the discrepancy between night-time experience and that of the day, strongly evoke the world of *A Midsummer Night's Dream*.

Virginia Woolf has created within her so-called 'traditional' novel a fiction of poetic intensity which explores complex psychological situations involving a spectrum of emotion from

VIRGINIA WOOLF AND THE POETRY OF FICTION

ecstasy to despair, and which draws on, and at times enacts, the subconscious dream world of fear and terror, and also a world of freedom and wish-fulfilment. The movement of Virginia Woolf's second novel is from the world of rational discourse and social convention to the irrational world of enchantment. Both modes of experience belong to what presents itself as the same surface world of mundane happenings and social intercourse. They belong together. It is through the one that the other is attained, and once attained it will function as the acknowledged social world of normality. The strange and mysterious lurk just below the surface of the habitual and the ordinary.

Chapter Three

THE POETIC NARRATIVE OF *JACOB'S ROOM*

Virginia Woolf's third novel is usually praised for its innovative structure: the traditional framework of the novel (plot structure) has suddenly been jettisoned, and a new kind of form has been used in which the narrative progresses, on the whole, through a series of impressionistic episodes that create the 'life' of Jacob Flanders. There are no connective narrative links between the episodes. The novel is generally criticized for its characterization: Jacob Flanders fails to come to life and is far too shadowy a figure. This twofold aspect of criticism, the exciting innovative nature of the novel's form on the one hand, and the inadequacy of the central character on the other, is justified on the terms in which the novel is usually approached, that is, either as the natural successor to *The Voyage Out* and *Night and Day* or as the precursor of *Mrs. Dalloway* and *To the Lighthouse.* On both counts it fails to satisfy. Too preoccupied with what *Jacob's Room* is not, critics have on the whole missed what that novel essentially is. It is essentially different from the two novels that preceded it and the two that followed it. It has been underestimated, in my opinion, because of a failure to grasp the originality of Virginia Woolf's new conception of a novel and the skill with which this new conception is realized. *Jacob's Room* is Virginia Woolf's most abstract and theoretic work yet its meaning is expressed poetically.

Jacob's Room is a novel of scepticism which challenges the nature of fiction itself and raises disturbing questions about the nature of human existence. At the centre of this intellectual exploration is the figure of Jacob Flanders. The book is not essentially about him in the way that, for instance, *Mrs.*

Dalloway is a book about Clarissa Dalloway, and the novel's title suggests that. It is a book rather, about the space, mental and physical, that is occupied by Jacob Flanders, the metaphoric 'room' that is his. It includes, for instance, his literal 'room' at Cambridge and also his rooms in Lamb's Conduit Street; at another level it is Cambridge, London, Paris, and Greece. And at another level again it is the metaphysical space nourished by Shakespeare, Homer, and Byron and often expressed in encounters with others, such as Bonamy, Durrant, or Florinda. The 'room', moreover, is also there when he is not, and in this sense the novel is about life itself, the life in which Jacob figures. This is true of the 'literal' rooms whose existence is described when Jacob is absent from them, and it is true also of the way in which London and Cambridge, in particular, are presented apart from him.

Jacob is encountered in a series of impressionist episodes, or fragments, and the book is about the fragmentation of life and the fragmentary nature of human experience. But the structure of the novel is still linear as in the traditional novel: it is as if episodes or significant moments have been selected from the whole story with all the connective narrative links removed from the plot framework of Jacob's *bildungsroman*. Virginia Woolf wrote that in *Jacob's Room* her approach would be very different from that of the preceding novels ('no scaffolding; scarcely a brick to be seen' *AWD*: 23), and that she wanted to 'get closer and yet keep form and speed'(ibid.). So *Jacob's Room* is a much shorter and more condensed work. Its structure is built up cumulatively through the juxtaposition of the episodes. Connections are made poetically, chiefly by the way in which images and motifs are picked up in different episodes and the way in which they become interwoven into the fabric of meaning. The meaning inheres in the poetic texture of the novel.

At the beginning of the novel Jacob's mother is on holiday with her children in Cornwall. A scene on the beach is created impressionistically from three different angles. First, the landscape is viewed through the distorting lens of Betty Flanders' tears: the scene before her dissolves before her eyes as the ink blot flows from her pen and marks the letter she is writing to

THE POETIC NARRATIVE OF *JACOB'S ROOM*

Captain Barfoot. The passage is effective through the play of words:

> Slowly welling from the point of her gold nib, pale blue ink dissolved the full stop; for there her pen stuck; her eyes fixed, and tears slowly filled them.
>
> (5)

The emergence of the ink is described in words usually associated with the forming of tears ('Slowly welling...'); and the forming of the tears in words which might apply to the spreading blot of ink ('tears slowly filled them'). Yet below the playfulness there is sorrow, as Betty Flanders reflects that it is two years since her husband died an accidental death, and she has to bring up three children on her own, one of whom, Jacob, is a difficult child. This is instanced by her response 'Well, if Jacob doesn't want to play...' and 'Where *is* that tiresome little boy?' (5). A little further on she reflects that 'Jacob is such a handful; so obstinate already'(9). Through her tears she sees the world awry as what is stable or fixed (the bay, the lighthouse) becomes unstable (the bay 'quivered', the lighthouse 'wobbled'). Life is precarious and nature can be destructive: the mast of the yacht bends 'like a wax candle in the sun'. The images in this passage are produced by distortion, yet they at the same time contain hints of the true nature of life. Mrs Flanders' reflection that 'Accidents were awful things'(5) stems from what she has seen of life's precariousness. Personal experience colours her outlook on life. So the novel opens with reference to a sense of bereavement; twenty years later she will again be bereaved when her son Jacob dies in the war. The book begins and ends with her personal loss.

The next impression is of a quite different nature. The viewpoint is that of an artist painting the scene before him with Betty Flanders at its centre (this prefigures Lily Briscoe's painting in *To the Lighthouse*). The impression created here is a visual one of balanced areas of colour, an impressionist painting:

> He struck the canvas a hasty violet-black dab. For the landscape needed it. It was too pale – greys flowing into

41

VIRGINIA WOOLF AND THE POETRY OF FICTION

lavenders, and one star or a white gull suspended just so –
too pale as usual.

(6)

The artist is working towards and eventually achieves, it seems,
a sense of unity, since he is pleased by 'the effect of the black
– it was just *that* note which brought the rest together'(7).
Throughout the novel as a whole there is an attempt, both by
the author and also by Jacob Flanders, to reach some kind of
meaning, and it is suggested (and this is true of all Virginia
Woolf's works) that meaning is only released when things have
come together, as with Lily Briscoe's picture at the end of *To
the Lighthouse* (when she is able to place her final stroke that
brings the whole together she can say 'I have had my vision' *TL*:
320), as with Rachel Vinrace's questioning ('Would there ever
be a time when the world was one and indivisible?' *VO*: 362).

It is the third impression that focuses more directly on
Jacob. His presence has been prepared for, however, particularly in the broken call of Archer to his wayward brother
'Ja-cob! Ja-cob!' from within the first two impressionistic fragments. The third such call is followed by an authorial comment
that voices the underlying pessimism of the novel:

> The voice had an extraordinary sadness. Pure from all body,
> pure from all passion, going out into the world, solitary,
> unanswered, breaking against rocks – so it sounded.

(7)

The innocent call of a child to his brother is thus universalized
into the melancholy voice of a doomed humanity, and it
prefigures the close of the novel. Jacob, for all his spirit and
optimism, is controlled by a deterministic universe.

The third impression with Jacob at its centre is bound up
with the rock which is literally there on the shore, but which
as a powerful symbol resonates through the whole text. The
rock is described realistically, but something beyond the literal
is at the same time implied:

> The rock was one of those tremendously solid brown, or
> rather black, rocks which emerge from the sand like
> something primitive.

(7)

THE POETIC NARRATIVE OF *JACOB'S ROOM*

From the top of this primitive-seeming object Jacob sees the 'primitive' sight which terrifies him: the man and woman stretched 'motionless, side by side' and described in terms that make them appear repulsive (they are 'enormous' and have 'large red faces'). And he runs away in a panic. His equilibrium is restored when he finds a sheep's skull (a nice piece of psychological realism, and Virginia Woolf is very good at conveying the way in which a child's mind works), and he carries off its jaw as a trophy; it is one of a cluster of images associated with death that spans the book. At the close of the day, and of this opening episode, Jacob is described in a way that suggests a figure in effigy. Asleep in his bed he looks 'profoundly unconscious. The sheep's jaw with the big yellow teeth in it lay at his feet'(12). The rock, in addition, contains the crab which sluggishly crawls along the bottom of its sandy pool, unable to move out of it. Catching it and placing it in his bucket Jacob also bears this away with him, and again, at the end of the day, the crab becomes a symbol of man's destiny, and of Jacob's in particular:

> The child's bucket was half-full of rainwater; and the opal-shelled crab slowly circled round the bottom, trying with its weakly legs to climb the steep side; trying again and falling back, and trying again and again.
>
> (12)

The crab trapped in the bucket also represents emblematically the dual movement of the novel: the tough, assertive, optimistic attempt of Jacob in particular trying symbolically to get to the top (especially in his climb on to the rock of the Acropolis), and the authorial narrative asserting pessimistically the power of a deterministic universe which constantly undermines human endeavour.

Less than a tenth of the novel is devoted to the childhood of Jacob Flanders, and what it reveals mostly about him is that he enjoys his own company, following solitary pursuits such as butterfly catching, and that he has a will of his own. As a small child he wanders off on his own to explore the world of the sea shore, and he shows his tenacity, or obstinacy, in clinging to the sheep's jaw after his mother has told him to throw it away. As an older boy, home on holiday from school, he will wander as far as eight miles from home in search of rare butterflies. He has the collector's enthusiasm and meticulous knowledge: 'The upper wings of the moth which Jacob held were undoubtedly marked with kidney-shaped spots of a fulvous hue. But there was no crescent upon the underwing' (21). One of his less attractive character traits which seems in no way to lessen as he grows up is his self-absorption. As a child, for instance, he takes himself off into the countryside, returning only after midnight, seemingly unconcerned that his mother has been upset and worried about him. He can be moody and even sulky with his Cambridge friends, and later in his relations with women he is chauvinistic and patronizing. On the whole I do not find his a very attractive personality. His friends like him.

One substantial chapter covers Jacob's years at Cambridge, and this is followed by a chapter given to his holiday spent with Timmy Durrant. And then the rest of the book, by far the greatest part of it (chapters V–XIV), concentrates on his life in London and includes his journey to Greece.

In Cambridge he searches intellectually for the meaning of life, and for something that will 'see him through' when he goes out into the 'real' world. But the ability of Cambridge to provide the kind of knowledge and wisdom that will endure and sustain after the enjoyment of college life is over is called into question authorially. Jacob's development is portrayed in narrative fragments which convey impressionistically different aspects of Cambridge life: social intercourse, learning, friendships, and so on. Through those fragments Virginia Woolf also builds up the 'room' which is Cambridge.

Jacob Flanders goes up to Cambridge in 1906 at the age of 19. The first glimpse of him is on the train journey in which he appears a self-absorbed young man, shy and clumsy, yet is courteous to the elderly lady travelling in the carriage with him. In the next fragment he is attending a service at King's College chapel, the author questioning the nature of the 'light' of Cambridge. The overall descriptive element in the chapel scene is that of the light. (The note of death at the centre of the episode calls into question the validity of that light.) On faces the marks of certainty and 'authority controlled by piety' (30) are detected. The chief characteristic

THE POETIC NARRATIVE OF *JACOB'S ROOM*

of the service is its beautiful ritual orderliness. The scene is described as if viewed through the lens of a roving camera; its final focus is on a particular undergraduate, Jacob Flanders, at the centre of the congregation. He looked 'extraordinarily vacant, his head thrown back, his hymn-book open at the wrong place'(30). The reader learns that the main source of his distraction is the presence of women in the chapel. He thinks they should not be there; he finds them 'as ugly as sin'(30). There is, therefore, no connection between the ordered beauty of the service in the ancient beautiful place and the mind of the young man in the congregation. The power and beauty neither of the place nor of the ritual impinge on his mind. He irreverently catches his friend's eye and winks at him. Clearly this particular 'light' so eloquently presented by the author fails to 'burn' for Jacob.

At the centre of this episode there are, however, two passages which through the poetic nature of the narrative reach beyond the surface level of the occasion itself.

An inclined plane of light comes accurately through each window, purple and yellow even in its most diffused dust, while, where it breaks upon stone, that stone is softly chalked red, yellow, and purple. Neither snow nor greenery, winter nor summer, has power over the old stained glass. As the sides of a lantern protect the flame so that it burns steady even in the wildest night – burns steady and gravely illumines the tree-trunks – so inside the Chapel all was orderly. Gravely sounded the voices; wisely the organ replied, as if buttressing human faith with the assent of the elements. The white-robed figures crossed from side to side; now mounted steps, now descended, all very orderly.

...If you stand a lantern under a tree every insect in the forest creeps up to it – a curious assembly, since though they scramble and swing and knock their heads against the glass, they seem to have no purpose – something senseless inspires them. One gets tired of watching them, as they amble round the lantern and blindly tap as if for admittance, one large toad being the most besotted of any and shouldering his way through the rest. Ah, but what's that? A terrifying volley of pistol-shots rings out – cracks

VIRGINIA WOOLF AND THE POETRY OF FICTION

sharply; ripples spread – silence laps smooth over sound. A tree – a tree has fallen, a sort of death in the forest. After that, the wind in the trees sounds melancholy.

(30)

The light that is 'purple and yellow even in its most diffused dust' suggests butterfly wings. In fact the words evoke such earlier specific descriptions as 'The pale clouded yellows had pelted over the moor; they had zigzagged across the purple clover' (22). They also connect with the specific episode from the past during which Jacob had gone off during the Easter holidays in search of butterflies. That occasion is then introduced into the narrative by an explicit allusion: 'As the sides of a lantern protect the flame...'. It is then recalled by Jacob and presented through his recollection of the occasion. What is particularly significant here technically is the manner of the recollection: Virginia Woolf goes through the actual psychological process of recall by which Jacob at first makes a conscious observation related to past experience ('If you stand a lantern under a tree every insect...') and then re-enacts the event which is thereby conveyed to the reader with the immediacy of experience ('Ah, but what's that? A terrifying volley of pistol-shots rings out...'). The 'curious assembly, of the forest' provides an ironic gloss on the assembly in the chapel. Most of the details of the original happening are embedded in the recollection of it during the chapel service, but an additional remark of major significance has been added as a gloss: 'a sort of death in the forest'. It is significant because it belongs to a cluster of images and observations which suggest that at the heart of life there is death. So, in this way, the childhood experience grows with the years as further meanings and implications attach themselves to it. The perspective alters. In Jacob's original reflection on his butterfly search it is the magic of the night and the beauty and fascination of the creatures that lingers in the mind even though the tree had fallen and the pistol-shots had been heard. In the college chapel the disturbing intrusion of death into the place of light and beauty is what is emphasized. It is emphasized further by a slight distortion of the facts. The night on which the tree had fallen had been a *windless* night. The record of

46

THE POETIC NARRATIVE OF *JACOB'S ROOM*

the event in the chapel scene reads:

> A tree – a tree has fallen, a sort of death in the forest. After
> that, the wind in the trees sounds melancholy.
>
> (30)

In the Cambridge section of the novel the tension between the
two polarities of Jacob, the individual on the one hand and his
room on the other becomes increasingly felt as he moves
steadily forward towards self-realization against the backward
tug of the authorial narrative which undermines his endeavour
through its tone of melancholy and its voice of scepticism.

Sunday lunch at the Plumers' is brilliantly presented in all
its boredom and futility. It sums up the emptiness of middle-
class ambition and pretension. Mrs Plumer grew up

> with an instinctively accurate notion of the rungs of the
> ladder and an ant-like assiduity in pushing George Plumer
> ahead of her to the top of the ladder. What was at the top
> of the ladder? A sense that all the rungs were beneath one
> apparently.
>
> (32–3)

The satire is directed at the social pretension which is
embodied in the don's wife. Mr Plumer, who is socially a bore,
possesses nevertheless an 'abstract light' in his cold grey eyes.
He can talk about Persia and the trade winds, the Reform Bill
and the cycle of harvests, but it is his socially climbing wife
who does most of the talking. Jacob is outraged by the occasion.
His response as he escapes from the house is emotional and
inarticulate: 'Oh God, oh God, oh God!' or 'Bloody beastly!' A
new light had been shed for him through this particular
glimpse of the life of the older generation whose false values
and meaningless lives he deplores. He has, of course, all the
arrogance of youth in his belief that he knows what life is and
where meaning and true values are to be found. 'Had they
never read Homer, Shakespeare, the Elizabethans?' (33)

Jacob's personal outburst is then objectified authorially into
the response of all youth, with its faith, optimism, and idealism,
to the 'world of the elderly'. What he has to pit against their
values is the accumulation of his own personal experience

VIRGINIA WOOLF AND THE POETRY OF FICTION

which represents 'reality' for him and which is symbolized by 'The moors and Byron; the sea and the lighthouse; the sheep's jaw with the yellow teeth in it' (34). In a summary way Virginia Woolf is here showing how from the accumulation of events in his youth (which have been described for the reader in the early sections of the novel), meaning has been extracted and will endure for the rest of his life. It is out of this accumulation that he forms his life. Life is not, as she writes in 'Modern Fiction', 'a series of gig lamps symmetrically arranged', it is 'a luminous halo, a semi-transparent envelope surrounding us from the beginning of consciousness to the end' (*CE*: 106). Jacob does not, in other words, move forward in his life leaving one phase of it behind him to go on to the next. The past *is* his life and he takes it forward with him so that enlarged and enriched it becomes the present, and everything is then carried forwards into the future so that his 'life' is something 'luminous' and continuous and whole. A major new note in this novel is the creation through the central character of an existential hero. Jacob moves step by step in the existential search for his own self, and this is underlined authorially in his response to the Plumers by the explicit and important claim Jacob makes and Virginia Woolf's gloss on it:

> 'I am what I am, and intend to be it,' for which there will be no form in the world unless Jacob makes one for himself.
>
> (34)

Reacting violently against the 'form' that the Plumers have made for themselves, he finds his in the natural surroundings of the river, the trees, grey spires, and the 'springy air of May'. It develops from, and will continue to develop from, Byron, Shakespeare, Homer, the moors, and his sheep's jaw.

Jacob's Cambridge is the Cambridge of Forster's *The Longest Journey* or of Thoby Stephen and Leonard Woolf, of what became the nucleus of 'Bloomsbury'. The social gatherings in the evenings in Jacob's room, or in the room of one of his friends where several of them talk and argue about history, or literature, or whatever ideas one or other was teasing out seem to have been what most influenced Jacob. Some friendships, chiefly those of Durrant and Bonamy (the 'good friend') survive and continue beyond Cambridge. Virginia Woolf

48

THE POETIC NARRATIVE OF *JACOB'S ROOM*

summarizes the friendship and companionability: 'It was the intimacy, a sort of spiritual suppleness, when mind prints upon mind indelibly' (44).

Jacob seeks for some kind of significance from history. "Does History consist in the Biographies of Great Men?" is the title of an essay he writes. His many historical interests include the Greeks (references to Homer, photographs of Greek sculpture, his Greek dictionary). But perhaps more significantly, he feels the influence of the past from the dignified ancient buildings around him. The place stands for the tradition of learning which enriches and ennobles the present: 'the sound of the clock conveying to him (it may be) a sense of old buildings and time; and himself the inheritor...' (43). So, apart from his own personal accumulation of knowledge and experience (Byron, the sheep's jaw, etc.) he is also the inheritor of the wisdom and knowledge of the past, or what part of it he is able to acquire and absorb.

At the end of the Cambridge chapter Jacob is universalized as 'the young man' in a way that makes his existence seem ephemeral compared to the buildings with their implied values that endure for centuries:

> Back from the Chapel, back from the Hall, back from the Library, came the sound of his footsteps, as if the old stone echoed with magisterial authority: "The young man – the young man – the young man – back to his rooms."
>
> (45)

Cambridge has been revealed to the reader in the human fabric through which its light must shine. Sopwith, for instance, with his verbal gymnastics and eloquence, will sound hollow to those sufficiently mature and perceptive to see through him. Yet with his wedges of chocolate cake young men are welcomed, and they grow articulate and acquire assurance as he encourages them to give shape to their thoughts. The household of the Professor of Physics is both literally and spiritually suburban. Huxtable with his capacious mind can be mean and petty about money. It is, however, through her portrait of Huxtable that Virginia Woolf pays tribute to scholarship at its highest, and the fragment in which he is portrayed is one which contains images that resonate later in the novel.

49

VIRGINIA WOOLF AND THE POETRY OF FICTION

Old Professor Huxtable, performing with the method of a
clock his change of dress, let himself down into his chair;
filled his pipe; chose his paper; crossed his feet; and
extracted his glasses. The whole flesh of his face then fell
into folds as if props were removed. Yet strip a whole seat of
an underground railway carriage of its heads and old
Huxtable's head will hold them all. Now, as his eye goes
down the print, what a procession tramps through the
corridors of his brain, orderly, quick-stepping, and
reinforced, as the march goes on, by fresh runnels, till the
whole hall, dome, whatever one calls it, is populous with
ideas. Such a muster takes place in no other brain. Yet
sometimes there he'll sit for hours together, gripping the
arm of the chair, like a man holding fast because stranded,
and then, just because his corn twinges, or it may be the
gout, what execrations, and, dear me, to hear him talk of
money, taking out his leather purse and grudging even the
smallest silver coin, secretive and suspicious as an old
peasant woman with all her lies. Strange paralysis and
constriction – marvellous illumination. Serene over it all
rides the great full brow, and sometimes asleep or in the
quiet spaces of the night you might fancy that on a pillow of
stone he lay triumphant.

(38)

Huxtable's head and the British Museum (chapter IX), for
instance, are linked allusively through the same kind of surreal
presentation:

There is in the British Museum an enormous mind.
Consider that Plato is there cheek by jowl with Aristotle; and
Shakespeare with Marlowe. This great mind is hoarded
beyond the power of any single mind to possess it.... A
learned man is the most venerable of all – a man like
Huxtable of Trinity, who writes all his letters in Greek, they
say, and could have kept his end up with Bentley. And then
there is science, pictures, architecture – an enormous mind.

The rain poured down. The British Museum stood in one
solid immense mound, very pale, very sleek in the rain, not
a quarter of a mile from him. The vast mind was sheeted

50

THE POETIC NARRATIVE OF *JACOB'S ROOM*

with stone; and each compartment in the depths of it was safe and dry....

Stone lies solid over the British Museum, as bone lies cool over the visions and heat of the brain. Only here the brain is Plato's brain and Shakespeare's....

(107–8)

Huxtable's capacious mind with its 'vast hall and dome' suggests a building like the British Museum. The British Museum, as the repository of the finest achievements of the greatest of the capacious minds from other cultures and throughout the centuries, resembles the capacious mind of Professor Huxtable. The playfulness of the imagery, carried over and expanded as it is in this instance from one episode to another, carries the thematic weight of the discussion of the nature of civilizations which is of central importance in this novel.

After the Cambridge section of the novel the perspective broadens out further, one result of this being a distancing of the reader from the central character as he gradually recedes within that perspective. The 'room' that is Jacob's comes under closer scrutiny, though he is there, of course, all the time, except in the last chapter when the room is literally and metaphorically empty.

The episode of Jacob's sailing holiday with Durrant forms a transition between the Cambridge and London sections of the novel. Centrally the episode is a simple and beautiful portrayal of friendship between young men. The culmination of the holiday is the awakening of idealized young love between Jacob and Clara, a love destined never to be fulfilled. The childhood and Cambridge years are the years of innocence; those of London the years of experience. London is mostly a testing-out ground for the ideas and ideals fostered through home, school, and university. In many of the situations in which he finds himself he tries to come to terms with what he recognizes as a discrepancy between his intellectual beliefs and the contradictory nature of 'real' life. The most elaborately explored of these is his affair with Florinda through which he is initiated into manhood and knowledge of the world.

In London, then, Jacob journeys from innocence to

51

experience, from youth to manhood. And then as a young man of 26 he dies in the war. His life is brief, and his achievement is, in the main, unremarkable. He has an unspecified office job, and in his spare time keeps up his literary pursuits, occasionally going to the British Museum to research items of particular interest. He moves in various circles from the Bohemian to the society world. In personal terms he keeps up with some of his college friends, and he becomes a womanizer. According to the specific instances revealed by the author he takes a mistress, has recourse to prostitutes, and finally falls in love with, or is seduced by, a married woman old enough to be his mother.

That, in factual terms, is his achievement. But although Jacob becomes an increasingly shadowy figure certain aspects of his inner development are closely monitored by the author, despite the fact that the reader is not allowed access to his deepest thoughts and feelings. Eventually he achieves a sense of self-realization. His literal and metaphoric journey to the Acropolis marks his arrival at a state of true self-identity. The moment is epiphanic:

> Jacob's intention was to sit down and read, and, finding a drum of marble conveniently placed, from which Marathon could be seen, and yet it was in the shade, while the Erechtheum blazed white in front of him, there he sat....
>
> And then looking up and seeing the sharp outline, his meditations were given an extraordinary edge; Greece was over; the Parthenon in ruins; yet there he was.

(149)

That is his real achievement.

London as the larger space into which Jacob moves after Cambridge is in many ways like the London of T. S. Eliot's *Waste Land*. There is, moreover, much in *Jacob's Room* that echoes Eliot's poem, both in the fragmentary nature of its structure and also in the sterile aspects of the 'unreal' city from which Jacob travels to Greece seeking an alternative to the sterility of western civilization. Ironically, as in Eliot's poem, one capital city turns out to be very like another. The

THE POETIC NARRATIVE OF *JACOB'S ROOM*

Greek myth is eventually exploded. There is no escape from the abyss for him, even in Athens:

> This gloom, this surrender to the dark waters which lap us about, is a modern invention. Perhaps, as Cruttendon said, we do not believe enough. Our fathers at any rate had something to demolish.
>
> (137)

The London sections of the novel begin with Jacob in his room in Lamb's Conduit Street looking up something in Virgil. The house in which he lives is an eighteenth-century house, and Virginia Woolf refers back to its earlier phase of existence. Then from this particular room, and house, and street, the narrative at once broadens out to create an impression of the city as a whole in which the individual is isolated and human beings do not communicate with each other:

> The proximity of the omnibuses gave the outside passengers an opportunity to stare into each other's faces. Yet few took advantage of it. Each had his own business to think of.
>
> (63)

One description of the London throng in particular evokes Eliot's crowd flowing over London Bridge, and Madame Sosostris's vision of the crowds walking round in a ring, all of which, of course, evoke allusively the damned who circle in Dante's hell.

> A homeless people, circling beneath the sky whose blue or white is held off by a ceiling cloth of steel filings and horse dung shredded to dust.
>
> (65)

Virginia Woolf's London is a sterile Modernist city.

Those who are essentially of the city are divorced from what is natural and life-enhancing, as in the humorous account of life in an office: 'upon each desk you observe, like provender, a bunch of papers, the day's nutriment, slowly consumed by the industrious pen' (65). London is 'the hoary city, old, sinful, and majestic' (66). Through it 'eternally the pilgrims trudge' (66). Virginia Woolf builds up poetically in this way an impression of a place that has a life of its own and which is also a human

VIRGINIA WOOLF AND THE POETRY OF FICTION

landscape, of search and endeavour at one extreme, of futility and emptiness at the other. The range between the two is vast and Jacob explores that range, which is the range of his 'room'. Various snippets scattered through the novel arrest the reader's attention and jerk him back to a realization of what kind of world Jacob inhabits. There is, for instance, the futility and repetitiveness of daily existence in the crowd that flows over Waterloo Bridge: 'All the time the stream of people never ceases passing from the Surrey side to the Strand; from the Strand to the Surrey side'(112). And that crowd is placed in the context of history: 'That old man has been crossing the Bridge these six hundred years...'(112). The city depersonalizes human beings: 'The women of the streets have the faces of playing cards; the outlines accurately filled in with pink and yellow, and the line drawn tightly round them'(114).

The 'night town' of Jacob's London is one of violence and unrest, an abyss that threatens, though the privileged are protected from its onslaught. Jacob walks through that world with Florinda:

> All night men and women seethed up and down the well-known beats. Late home-comers could see shadows against the blinds even in the most respectable suburbs....
>
> The voices, angry, lustful, despairing, passionate, were scarcely more than the voices of caged beasts at night. Only they are not caged, nor beasts. Stop a man; ask him the way; he'll tell it you; but one's afraid to ask him the way. What does one fear? – the human eye. At once the pavement narrows, the chasm deepens. There! They've melted into it – both man and woman. Farther on, blatantly advertising its meritorious solidity, a boarding-house exhibits behind uncurtained windows its testimony to the soundness of London. There they sit, plainly illuminated, dressed like ladies and gentlemen, in bamboo chairs. The widows of business men prove laboriously that they are related to judges. The wives of coal merchants instantly retort that their fathers kept coachmen. A servant brings coffee, and the crochet basket has to be moved. And so on again into the dark, passing a girl here for sale, or there an old woman

THE POETIC NARRATIVE OF *JACOB'S ROOM*

with only matches to offer, passing the crowd from the Tube
station, the women with veiled hair, passing at length no
one but shut doors, carved door-posts, and a solitary
policeman, Jacob, with Florinda on his arm, reached his
room and, lighting the lamp, said nothing at all.

(78, 80–1)

Jacob trustingly walks through that world with Florinda, succumbing to her sensual charms, and naïvely believing in her
innocence. As he makes his way through that landscape he
journeys towards the knowledge that comes from experience.

London is a microcosm of the universe. Many images of
society reinforce and reveal aspects of that microcosm. One
such is the opera house which, through the arrangement of its
seating, links together a sense of the isolation of the individual
and the class structure by which people are categorized within
a hierarchy:

Only to prevent us from being submerged by chaos, nature
and society between them have arranged a system of
classification which is simplicity itself; stalls, boxes,
amphitheatre, gallery.

(67)

Although the focus of the image here is on the privileged
society world, it none the less reveals that no amount of
privilege can protect man from the spirit of the age, 'for
wherever I seat myself, I die in exile'(68).

In his pilgrimage through this city Jacob succeeds in establishing a certain continuity in his life which gives to it a kind
of unity. This is suggested at the surface level, for instance, in
the contents of his room where items from the past find a
place beside things of the present: 'The furniture – three
wicker chairs and a gate-legged table – came from Cambridge'(69). But it is above all in his continuing preoccupation
with the Greeks that he builds up the 'form' of his life. They
are at the centre of his journey towards selfhood, and his
pilgrimage ends on the rock of the Acropolis. It was in Cambridge that he became imbued with the 'spirit of the Greeks',
and this continually influences his thought and behaviour in
London. This is also humorously and seriously exploited by

the author as she constructs the metaphysical world or 'room' whereby she ultimately forces the reader to face the state of western civilization when Europe is on the brink of war in the summer of 1914. But the preoccupation with the Greeks is, to begin with, of a much more light-hearted nature.

As a young man of 22 Jacob is, outwardly at least, assured and boastful, and very handsome. At a Guy Fawkes party his manly beauty is acknowledged when he is garlanded and honoured as a Greek god: 'So they wreathed his head with paper flowers. Then somebody brought out a white and gilt chair and made him sit on it. As they passed, people hung glass grapes on his shoulders...'(74). And on his way home in the small hours he discusses the Greeks with Durrant:

> Durrant quoted Aeschylus — Jacob Sophocles... it seemed to both that they had read every book in the world; known every sin, passion and joy. Civilizations stood round them like flowers ready for picking. Ages lapped at their feet like waves fit for sailing. And surveying all this, looming through the fog, the lamplight, the shades of London, the two young men decided in favour of Greece.
>
> "Probably," said Jacob, "we are the only people in the world who know what the Greeks meant."
>
> (74–5)

Yet this fairly simple reference to the Greeks conveys more than the ebullience of the boastful and contented young men who have so obviously been enjoying themselves. The fore-grounded elegant statement

> Civilizations stood round them like flowers ready for picking. Ages lapped at their feet like waves fit for sailing.

places Jacob and his attitudes in a more general perspective by drawing attention to the wider social and cultural nature of his 'journey' through London. These lines are an interesting example of how the poetic discourse of the novel creates a multi-layered narrative from within a simple one. They suggest related alternatives, the one historical and the other cultural, for investigation by a young man perplexed by the world he finds himself in at the close of the Edwardian era. But the author does not leave it at that. There follows a long authorial

THE POETIC NARRATIVE OF *JACOB'S ROOM*

passage which begins in the style of the familiar essay and concludes with one of those almost choric statements of brooding melancholy that emphasize the ultimately doomed nature of human endeavour.

> A strange thing – when you come to think of it – this love of Greek, flourishing in such obscurity, distorted, discouraged, yet leaping out, all of a sudden, especially on leaving crowded rooms, or after a surfeit of print, or when the moon floats among the waves of the hills, or in hollow, sallow, fruitless London days, like a specific; a clean blade; always a miracle. Jacob knew no more Greek than served him to stumble through a play. Of ancient history he knew nothing. However, as he tramped into London it seemed to him that they were making the flagstones ring on the road to the Acropolis, and that if Socrates saw them coming he would bestir himself and say 'my fine fellows', for the whole sentiment of Athens was entirely after his heart; free, venturesome, high-spirited... She [Florinda] had called him Jacob without asking his leave. She had sat upon his knee. Thus did all good women in the days of the Greeks.
>
> At this moment there shook out into the air a wavering, quavering, doleful lamentation which seemed to lack strength to unfold itself, and yet flagged on; at the sound of which doors in back streets burst sullenly open; workmen stumped forth.
>
> (75)

The metaphoric journey referred to here ('making the flag-stones ring on the road to the Acropolis') anticipates the later literal journey to Greece. A further gloss on the nature of the peculiarly English understanding of the Greeks is to be found in Virginia Woolf's essay 'On Not Knowing Greek' (*CR* I). One of its more telling comments, which reinforces Jacob's interest in the Greeks, is that

> They [the Greeks] admit us to a vision of the earth unravaged, the sea unpolluted, the maturity, tried but unbroken, of mankind.... Back and back we are drawn to steep ourselves in what, perhaps, is only an image of the

57

VIRGINIA WOOLF AND THE POETRY OF FICTION

reality, not the reality itself, a summer's day imagined in the heart of a northern winter.

(*CR* I: 54–5)

In the conclusion of the essay Virigina Woolf expresses sentiments similar to those of the older Jacob who goes to Greece out of a need to find something better than what his own culture has to offer: 'and it is to the Greeks that we turn when we are sick of the vagueness, of the confusion, of the Christianity and its consolations, of our own age' (*CR* I: 58).

In lighter vein, the Greek theme is built up through comparisons, often playful, in which several people are described or viewed by reference to the Greeks. Jacob admires Florinda: 'Wild and frail and beautiful she looked, and thus the women of the Greeks were, Jacob thought...'(77). And later, observing Sandra Wentworth Williams, he is struck by her beauty: 'for hers was the English type which is so Greek...'(141). Florinda tells Jacob that he looks like one of the statues in the British Museum(79). Four years later Fanny Elmer who has been deserted by Jacob goes regularly to the British Museum to 'reinforce her vision' of him by gazing upon a statue:

> keeping her eyes downcast until she was alongside of the battered Ulysses, she opened them and got a fresh shock of Jacob's presence, enough to last her half a day.
>
> (170)

More prophetically, however, it is the statue of Achilles (not the triumphant Ulysses), a memorial to the dead, that suggests Jacob's fate:

> The loop of the railing beneath the statue of Achilles was full of parasols and waistcoats....
> " 'This statue was erected by the women of England...' "
> Clara read out with a foolish little laugh.
>
> (167)

The reference is then repeated, but in an extended form which leaves the reader in no doubt about the impending war and what its outcome will be:

> Yet five minutes after she [Julia Eliot] had passed the statue of Achilles she had the rapt look of one brushing through

THE POETIC NARRATIVE OF *JACOB'S ROOM*

crowds on a summer's afternoon, when the trees are
rustling, the wheels churning yellow, and the tumult of the
present seems like an elegy for past youth and past
summers, and there rose in her mind a curious sadness, as if
time and eternity showed through skirts and waistcoats, and
she saw people passing tragically to destruction.

(168)

Jacob had seen Clara as 'a virgin chained to a rock (somewhere
off Lowndes Square) eternally pouring out tea.... Of all women,
Jacob honoured her most' (122). But he does not play Perseus
to her Andromeda. Had he lived longer he, presumably, would
have done so. But we cannot be sure of that. Plato's argument
takes a hold on Jacob as he reads the *Phaedrus* late into the
night:

And so, when at length one reads straight ahead, falling into
step, marching on, becoming (so it seems) momentarily
part of this rolling, imperturbable energy, which has driven
darkness before it since Plato walked the Acropolis, it is
impossible to see to the fire.
The dialogue draws to its close. Plato's argument is done.
Plato's argument is stowed away in Jacob's mind, and for
five minutes Jacob's mind continues alone, onwards, into
the darkness.

(108–9)

The *Phaedrus*, however, is about death and the immortality of
the soul, so that despite the humorous way in which Virginia
Woolf describes Jacob's reading, an ominous note is sounded;
the narrative becomes increasingly pessimistic once Jacob has
gone to Greece.

Virginia Woolf's elaborate exploration of the Greeks unifies
the historical, cultural, and spiritual themes of the novel as it
moves towards a serious consideration of the significance of
the history and culture of the past both in the emergence of
the individual in the modern world and as a means of confronting the decline of western civilization as Europe moves
closer to war. The two aspects interlock in Jacob's destiny
which had been poetically expressed in an authorial comment

59

VIRGINIA WOOLF AND THE POETRY OF FICTION

on Jacob as he sat gloomily looking at Land's End during his
sailing holiday with Durrant:

> We start transparent, and then the cloud thickens. All
> history backs our pane of glass. To escape is vain.
>
> (47)

Personal history, despite individual personal endeavour, is
controlled by destiny, the unfolding of history, and the development of civilizations. The civilization that nurtures Jimmy
Dawes and Jacob Flanders is the civilization that condones the
war that destroys them. Jimmy's fate ('And now Jimmy feeds
crows in Flanders and Helen visits hospitals' 95–6) anticipates
Jacob's fate.

As a younger man, Jacob's attitude had been 'Detest your
own age. Build a better one'(106) and the Greeks were his
ideal. With a sense of urgency he writes to Bonamy from
Greece:

> I intend to come to Greece every year so long as I live....
> It is the only chance I can see of protecting oneself from
> civilization.
>
> (145)

But he discovers that Greece is finished, and the myth an
illusion. The authorial voice explains: 'But it is the governesses
who start the Greek myth.... The point is, however, that we
have been brought up in an illusion'(136). Jacob realizes as he
looks down on Marathon and out to the Isles of Greece that
Greece is 'over' and the Parthenon in ruins (149).

As Jacob dreams and lives out his dreams in Greece, Europe
is gathering her forces for war.

> The battleships ray out over the North Sea, keeping their
> stations accurately apart.... Like blocks of tin soldiers the
> army covers the cornfield, moves up the hillside, stops, reels
> slightly this way and that, and falls flat, save that, through
> field-glasses, it can be seen that one or two pieces still
> agitate up and down like fragments of broken match-stick.
>
> (155)

Jacob's 'pilgrimage', charted largely in terms of the Greeks, is
accomplished when he reaches the Acropolis. Yet despite his

THE POETIC NARRATIVE OF *JACOB'S ROOM*

epiphany there the voice of authorial scepticism questions the success of his symbolic journey:

> As for reaching the Acropolis who shall say that we ever do it, or that when Jacob woke next morning he found anything hard and durable to keep for ever?

(160)

In the authorial transition back to London from Greece the narrative makes more explicit the precariousness of man's position and doubts his ability to survive the chaotic forces that will soon overwhelm him in the European war. The wind 'rolling the darkness through the streets of Athens' heralds the storm that is brewing in Europe. The questions raised by Virginia Woolf in this slight book are profound and far-reaching; mostly they are raised in an unobtrusive manner, and mostly they lie below the bright and entertaining surface of the book.

Even though *Jacob's Room* is a much more intellectual, theoretical novel than any of her others, its impact is finally achieved through its poetic narrative. What lingers in the mind, after the authorial dialectic has been teased out and the novel's underpinning structure has been observed, stems from the twofold aspect of that poetic narrative; first in the images which subsume the novel's major themes, such as the sheep's skull, the name Flanders and the pressed poppies, Greek sculpture and butterflies, and, in the end, a pair of old shoes. Reinforcing this is the other, the elegiac authorial narrative, drawing attention to the precariousness of life in its melancholy and sceptical intrusions. The melancholy voice heard in the scene on the beach at the beginning of the novel – 'The voice had an extraordinary sadness. Pure from all body, pure from all passion, going out into the world, solitary, unanswered, breaking against rocks – so it sounded' (7) – is the ground base of the novel which is Virginia Woolf's elegy for Jacob and for all the young men who died in the Great War.

Chapter Four

THE RHYTHMIC ORDER OF
MRS. DALLOWAY

Mrs. Dalloway is a completely unified novel. Its unity is achieved in large measure through its texture: the density of the writing, and the devices and techniques by which the whole is enriched and given a seamless quality. Of major significance is the cluster of images by which the author reaches from the outer world to the inner and which, through its recurrent patterning, creates the 'rhythmic order' of the novel.

In *A Room of One's Own* Virginia Woolf describes an ordinary London scene such as one might see in looking down from an upper window.

> At this moment, as so often happens in London, there was a complete lull and suspension of traffic. Nothing came down the street; nobody passed. A single leaf detached itself from the plane tree at the end of the street, and in that pause and suspension fell. Somehow it was like a signal falling, a signal pointing to a force in things which one had overlooked. It seemed to point to a river, which flowed past invisibly, round the corner, down the street, and took people and eddied them along, as the stream at Oxbridge had taken the undergraduate in his boat and the dead leaves. Now it was bringing from one side of the street to the other diagonally a girl in patent leather boots, and then a young man in a maroon overcoat; it was bringing a taxi-cab; and it brought all three together at a point beneath my window; where the taxi stopped, and the girl and the young man stopped; and they got into the taxi; and then the cab glided off as if it were swept on by the current elsewhere.

> (*AROO:* 144–5)

THE RHYTHMIC ORDER OF *MRS. DALLOWAY*

What is being suggested here is that within such everyday scenes as this, there is something extraordinary, below the surfaces of things, to be discovered. She calls it 'a force in things' and likens it to an invisible river that can sweep along streets and round corners and 'eddy' people along on it. Her own gloss on her strange way of experiencing such a scene is that 'The sight was ordinary enough; what was strange was the rhythmic order with which my imagination had invested it' (*AROO*: 145). In this imagined scene, then, the reader is presented with both the ordinary sight of what happened and a 'rhythmic order' investing it; the 'imagined' scene is like a miniature of the novel *Mrs. Dalloway.*

Much of *Mrs. Dalloway* is built out of this odd mixture of the ordinary and the strange. What is 'ordinary' is the scene, the people, the happenings. In fact everything that makes up the June day in London, which forms in one sense the substance of the book, is ordinary. What is 'strange' is the vitality and mystery that is being continually revealed within or below ordinary things. One of the ways in which Virginia Woolf reaches below the surface of the day, and its events that have been realistically created with convincing particularity, is through the 'rhythmic order' with which her imagination has invested it.

The 'rhythmic order' as a technique of penetrating to the larger reality behind the ordinary is expressed through the 'ebb and flow' of the life that is both within the individual and also outside him like the river in the passage from *A Room of One's Own* in which the young people getting into the taxi are caught up. The main characters of *Mrs. Dalloway* are similarly caught up in the current, or the 'ebb and flow' of life, and it is through its steady rhythmic presence that their separate lives are gauged, connected, and a structure of meaning is built up in the novel. The river, the current, the wave, the sea, the ebb and flow, running water, form a cluster of images related to the 'force in things' which draws the attention of the reader to the 'rhythmic order' that both controls and expresses life.

The novel is set in London. Yet in its opening pages the atmosphere and feel of that June day is first of all suggested through images associated with the sea. The June morning is fresh 'as if issued to children on a beach', and Clarissa Dalloway 'plunges' into the morning to make her way to the florist. She also 'plunges' into her past and remembers how she had 'plunged into the open air' at Bourton. The place of Clarissa's past recalled in the opening of the novel is not by the sea, and neither has it any connection with the sea. Bourton is in the country, and whenever Peter Walsh thinks of Clarissa it is usually as she was at Bourton and walking through woods and fields. Yet as Clarissa in her interior monologue recalls details of Bourton in the summer, remembering the air, the trees, and the birds, they are all described in terms of their movement or rhythm which is that of the wave. The air at Bourton, more still than the air in London on this June morning, was 'like the flap of a wave; the kiss of a wave'(5), and the rooks were 'rising, falling'. It is, however, not so much the actual setting that is made vivid by the sea imagery, but a remembered feeling about life that Clarissa had had when she was eighteen at Bourton. What the passage focuses on, in other words, once the setting and atmosphere have been established, is a poignant 'moment' from the past. The chill and sharpness of the air that is remembered is what she had been aware of when standing at an open window in the early morning, and it is associated with a chill and sharp feeling she then had that something awful was about to happen. The moment was 'solemn' because it was a moment in which a decision was about to be made that would determine the course that her life would take. That particular summer she refused Peter Walsh and accepted Richard Dalloway. None of this is stated at this stage in the novel. Clarissa merely reflects that one of these days Peter Walsh will be returning from India, and she recalls his sayings. As the novel unfolds, and her refusal of Peter Walsh is examined from several points of view, the reader realizes retrospectively why Bourton, seemingly casually mentioned on the first page of the novel, is of such significance. The significance had, however, been signalled by Virginia Woolf through the 'rhythmic order' with which she had invested the memory. The 'wave' images somehow indicate the 'force in things' at the source of the memory, though what Clarissa is most conscious of is the detail of what is associated

THE RHYTHMIC ORDER OF *MRS. DALLOWAY*

with that 'force' in her life. Virginia Woolf cuts across those details to indicate the underlying controlling irrevocability of her past by investing the scene and the memory with a rhythmic order.

Throughout the June day which forms the time-scale of the novel, Clarissa's emotional temperature is charted: it follows a rising and falling movement in which she alternately feels caught up in and afloat on life, or in the depths and over-whelmed by it. Mostly, in the course of the novel, she is looking inwards. Her inner self can lose its serenity, and the most insistent moments in which this happens, and she feels overwhelmed by life, are the occasions in which she feels threat or rejection or that there is not a great deal of life left for her to live. Her negative feelings of hate for Miss Kilman who has such a strong emotional hold on Elizabeth, for example, or the sense of rejection she feels when Peter Walsh tells her that he is in love with a young woman in India (in love, that is, with someone other than herself), or the feeling of being excluded when Lady Bruton asked her husband, Richard, to lunch but not herself, can all cause her to feel insecure and 'plunged' into the depths. Equally she can be, as it were, brought back to the surface of life by pleasant en-counters that restore and reassure her. Miss Pym's liking her, for instance, or her awareness that her servants respect and appreciate her, is sufficient to dispel her dark thoughts. Life going on around her, particularly in the London streets, can also rescue her from her sense of the isolation of her self, though her sense of the continuing life going on outside her can also, paradoxically, make her feel outside life. The rising and falling movement of all these powerful feelings, and the whole of life, the inner and the outer, which is at times experienced with insistence or intensity in the course of the day, is indicated by the rhythmic order asserting itself to reveal the 'force of life'. Usually that rhythmic order is con-veyed by the establishing of a definite rhythmic movement, or in one or more of the 'sea' images that presuppose the rhythmic and mythic force of the sea as an archetypal symbol of life.

The outer life of the London scene has a vitality of its own. Virginia Woolf has created a sense of its vitality through a

VIRGINIA WOOLF AND THE POETRY OF FICTION

patterned rhythmic prose which bears the reader along energetically by its force:

> In people's eyes, in the swing, tramp, and trudge; in the
> bellow and the uproar; the carriages, motor cars,
> omnibuses, vans; sandwich men shuffling and swinging;
> brass bands; barrel organs; in the triumph and the jingle
> and the strange high singing of some aeroplane overhead
> was what she loved; life; London; this moment of June.
>
> (6)

In this passage different kinds of movement, of noise, of vehicles, objects, and people are all tumbled out in no kind of logical order, though the listing does fall on the ear with an easy and jolly rhythm. The items all add up to the kind of life one experiences in the busy centre of London. Clarissa, who is responding enthusiastically to this outer scene, comments on how she loves this life: 'how one sees it so, making it up, building it round one, tumbling it, creating it every moment afresh....' It is as if, therefore, Virginia Woolf has herself 'tumbled' it out, creating it afresh, and built it round Clarissa. The prose exactly represents Clarissa's excited way of seeing it at this particular moment and in a particular frame of mind.

The sense of movement in the London that Clarissa is responding to is like the 'current of life' that swept up the young people getting into the taxi, in the scene from *A Room of One's Own*. And the expected image is slipped in imperceptibly as the reader is told that London is caught up 'brilliantly, on waves of that divine vitality which Clarissa loved' (9). Yet as Clarissa is looking at the taxicabs, and finding the bustle absorbing, she suddenly has a sense of 'being out, out, far out to sea and alone; she always had the feeling that it was very, very dangerous to live even one day' (11). Clarissa believes that after death she will still be part of this outer life, and its stream that bears one up and on:

> that somehow in the streets of London, on the ebb and flow
> of things, here, there, she survived ... being laid out like a
> mist between the people she knew best, who lifted her on
> their branches as she had seen the trees lift the mist....
>
> (11–12)

66

THE RHYTHMIC ORDER OF *MRS. DALLOWAY*

Clarissa is caught up in the rhythmic flow of life, and she is an onlooker reflecting on that life which is outside her but in which she is inextricably bound.

The Bond Street section of the novel reaches its climax in the florist's. Clarissa had entered the shop with a disturbing feeling of dislike for Miss Kilman. The 'brute' hatred would any moment 'be stirring, this hatred, which, especially since her illness, had power to make her feel scraped, hurt in her spine'. Once in the shop, however, and influenced by the coolness and beauty around her and the warmth of Miss Pym, her anguish is gradually dispelled. It is a sense of life that is rescuing her, and this is conveyed through the image of the wave that is more powerful than the monster that is disturbing her, attacking her in her soul.

> And she began to go with Miss Pym from jar to jar, choosing
> ... as if this beauty, this scent, this colour, and Miss Pym
> liking her, trusting her, were a wave which she let flow over
> her and surmount that hatred, that monster, surmount it
> all; and it lifted her up and up....
>
> (16)

When Clarissa feels rejected at not being invited to Lady Bruton's luncheon, life is at once felt to be overwhelming. Her feelings are conveyed by the now familiar image of life, but here it has associations of coldness and vulnerability:

> for the shock of Lady Bruton asking Richard to lunch
> without her made the moment in which she had stood
> shiver, as a plant on the river-bed feels the shock of a
> passing oar and shivers: so she rocked: so she shivered.
>
> (34)

What the message actually makes her feel is the dwindling of life. The coldness is the threat of time that would separate her from Richard, in death. Lady Bruton's momentary taking him away from her is, as it were, a portent of this. The sunny June morning had made her feel mostly caught up and involved in life. Now she feels that her grasp on life is precarious: she can be rocked as easily as a plant on the river-bed. As she is comparing her dwindling life (she is fifty-three and has been ill) with the full life of her youthful years when she was able to

67

absorb 'the colours, salts, tones of existence', she recalls those feelings as they would have come to her on entering a drawing-room, an action and an occasion which is itself symbolic of life. Virginia Woolf embodies those momentary feelings of suspense on the threshold of a drawing-room in the image of a diver plunging into the waves. Clarissa remembers

> an exquisite suspense, such as might stay a diver before plunging while the sea darkens and brightens beneath him, and the waves which threaten to break, but only gently split their surface, roll and conceal and encrust as they just turn over the weeds with pearl.
>
> (34–5)

Common to both images, the plant on the river-bed and the diver plunging into the sea, is the element of water which is expressive of life. The one image conveys delight and the other fear. The plant on the river-bed, submerged and fixed in life, feels the vibrations through the water of what is passing it by and is potentially a threat to it. But it can do no more than react to this by registering the fear and unease it feels by 'shivering'. The plant is imprisoned, stuck in life. This is how Clarissa feels about life in the moments in which she thinks of her age and her health. It is now necessary for her to rest in the afternoons and to sleep alone in order to have undisturbed nights. These are the facts of her dwindling life that induce dark thoughts, and are the reason why she is more easily buffeted by life. The 'plant' has not the resilience or the vitality of the 'diver' who can freely and spontaneously plunge into life.

The other image, of the younger years of sheer delight in life, recalls the Clarissa who was vital and free-moving. The diver plunges into the sea as she had 'plunged' into the air at Bourton, but also as she had 'plunged' into the freshness of the morning earlier in this present June day. The free spirit still, in fact, has a hold in the older Clarissa, and it will be felt most strongly at the party at the end of the day. The description of the waves into which the diver plunges is full of gentleness and light and beauty. Although the waves threaten to break, they merely ripple playfully and caressingly over the weeds, and the water 'brightens' to receive the diver. Life can be kind

THE RHYTHMIC ORDER OF *MRS. DALLOWAY*

and soothing. But as Clarissa is locked in her moment of introspection she looks deeper into her own life and recalls moments of failure, of how she had failed Richard through some contraction of her 'cold spirit'. She sees the failure in herself as a lack of a life-enhancing or life-bestowing element, the effect of which in relationships is similar to the effect of the waves.

It was something central which permeated; something warm which broke up surfaces and rippled the cold contact of man and woman, or of women together.

(36)

The belief that life can, indeed, be soothing and kind is restored to Clarissa as she senses that her servants appreciate her, and as she begins to think about the party, going to her cupboard to select her evening dress. By the time she has reached her drawing-room and is sitting on the sofa mending that dress, she is calm and content. The action of sewing, as 'her needle, drawing the silk smoothly to its gentle pause, collected the green folds together and attached them, very lightly, to the belt,'(44) is soothing. It is like the action of waves gathering on the shore. Her dress is for the party, and the party is the occasion on which she symbolically 'plunges' into life. The connection had been made earlier as she took her evening dress from the cupboard, 'plunging' her hand into its softness. The dress is green. Peter Walsh seeing her walk past in her 'silver-green' dress at the party thinks of mermaids lolloping on the waves. The connection between the folds of the dress and the waves of the sea, suggesting the return to positive thoughts, is made explicitly as Clarissa is sewing. The sea imagery here does not suggest the exquisite thrill and excitement of the moment of 'plunging' into the darkening and brightening waters, though it is still connected indirectly with it, for Clarissa will experience it again at the end of the day.

This is a moment of calm preparation, a distant anticipation of the symbolic occasion of the party, but the serenity that Clarissa feels is connected with the party. So instead of 'plunging' into the waters she is, symbolically, lying on a beach listening to the soothing rhythms of the waves breaking, as she

69

VIRGINIA WOOLF AND THE POETRY OF FICTION

is quietly preparing for her party. Now she is able to shed her anxieties and troubles; life which takes them over restores and sustains her by its gentle continuance:

> the heart, committing its burden to some sea, which sighs collectively for all sorrows, and renews, begins, collects, lets fall.
>
> (45)

Peter Walsh breaks into this reverie and disturbs Clarissa's serenity, when, in the course of their conversation he tells her that he is 'in love with a girl in India'. Clarissa counters her sense of rejection by fighting on against it in her own consciousness. The 'force' that asserts itself within her is like a river urging her on.

> But the indomitable egotism which for ever rides down the hosts opposed to it, the river which says on, on, on; even though, it admits, there may be no goal for us whatever, still on, on; this indomitable egotism charged her cheeks with colour; made her look very young; very pink; very bright-eyed as she sat with her dress upon her knee, and her needle held to the end of green silk, trembling a little.
>
> (50–1)

The sitting still and trembling a little recalls the image of the plant on the river-bed which embodied Clarissa's feelings of rejection when Lady Bruton had asked Richard to lunch without her. The shock of the 'passing oar' which disturbed it caused it to shiver: 'so it rocked; so it shivered'. In both instances it is life itself that goes on, and urges one, Clarissa feels, not to succumb to its blows. Clarissa's feelings are not stated; they are embodied in the images which vary and adapt to reveal the adjustment that the consciousness is continually making to life with its demands, its harshnesses, and its capacity to soothe.

Richard Dalloway returns home unexpectedly in the middle of the afternoon; three o'clock is striking. Clarissa, who is sitting at her writing table, is annoyed at having to ask Ellie Henderson to her party, and is concerned about the hold that Miss Kilman has on her daughter, Elizabeth. Her mixed feelings of unease are reflected in the way in which she now hears the sound of the hour striking.

THE RHYTHMIC ORDER OF *MRS. DALLOWAY*

And the sound of the bell flooded the room with its
melancholy wave; which receded, and gathered itself
together to fall once more, when she heard, distractingly,
something fumbling, something scratching at the door... the
door handle slipped round and in came Richard!

(130)

Richard's surprise visit lifts her gloom, though not immediately.
He leaves as the clock is striking the half-hour. By that time
Clarissa's sense of the melancholy note in the sound flooding
her room has been dispelled.

There is, however, something 'solemn' for Clarissa in the
way in which Big Ben strikes the half-hour. The solemnity in
this instance is primarily associated with the old lady at her
window whom Clarissa catches sight of as the clock is striking.
But in addition Clarissa has, since she has been ill, felt a
'solemnity', an indescribable pause – 'that might be her heart,
affected, they said, by influenza'(6) – before Big Ben strikes.
The old lady moves away from the window 'as if she were
attached to that sound'; the sound which descends into the
midst of ordinary things 'like a finger' makes the moment
solemn. There is a sense of mystery in the old lady's independence and privacy which profoundly affects and influences
Clarissa:

that's the miracle, that's the mystery; that old lady, she
meant, whom she could see going from chest of drawers to
dressing-table. ... And the supreme mystery which Kilman
might say she had solved, or Peter might say he had solved,
but Clarissa didn't believe either of them had the ghost of
an idea of solving, was simply this: here was one room; there
another. Did religion solve that, or love?

(140–1)

In this 'solemn' moment several things have come together
and fused: the sound of Big Ben, thoughts on love and religion,
the old lady. Clarissa is trying to work out for herself something about the perplexing nature of life itself. Miss Kilman
tries intellectually, and through religion, to find answers to
life's problems, and Richard tries to solve some problems by

71

VIRGINIA WOOLF AND THE POETRY OF FICTION

Acts of Parliament and by sitting on committees. Clarissa is weighing alternatives: she finds a greater reality in what the solitary old lady represents as she goes quietly about her business; she respects her independence and her privacy of soul. But Clarissa is jerked out of these profound thoughts by remembering mundane things that need to be attended to, 'Mrs Marsham, Ellie Henderson, glasses for ices. She must telephone now at once'(141). Both preoccupations, however, the one with the unfathomable mystery of life, and the other with the physical and practical details of ordinary day-to-day living, are part and parcel of the same 'life' that sustains one in its ebb and flow. This often disconcerting complexity of life, at once 'solemn' like the authoritative sound of Big Ben and banal like that clock that comes in on its wake 'with its lap full of trifles', is suggested in the images of the all-embracing sea that Virginia Woolf builds into her fanciful description of the clocks.

> Love – but here the other clock, the clock which always struck two minutes after Big Ben, came shuffling in with its lap full of odds and ends, which it dumped down as if Big Ben were all very well with his majesty laying down the law, so solemn, so just, but she must remember all sorts of little things besides – Mrs. Marsham, Ellie Henderson, glasses for ices – all sorts of little things came flooding and lapping and dancing in on the wake of that solemn stroke which lay flat like a bar of gold on the sea.
>
> (141)

Imagery fuses metaphysical preoccupations and the routine dailiness of life. The duration of the day is marked naturally by the ebb and flow of the tides, and mechanically by the clocks, each of which provides one of life's most insistent rhythms. The image of the stroke of the half-hour as a bar of gold lying on the waters unites the two. The pattern of complex thought and feeling that can be traced in Clarissa's consciousness in the last few moments of this episode are condensed and simplified in the image of the sea.

This is the last scene in which Clarissa is physically present in the novel before the party, and echoes from it and her moment of awareness are heard during the party. Clarissa,

THE RHYTHMIC ORDER OF *MRS. DALLOWAY*

who retires from the throng of the party to the little room in order to reflect on the suicide of Septimus Warren Smith, looks out of the window. The old lady who is at her window looks across at Clarissa; and Clarissa looking at the sky thinks 'It will be a solemn sky'. And as she hears the clock striking she leaves her private thoughts to return to the world in which she 'must assemble'(204–5). Leaving personal reflection to return to the party is similar to the way in which, in the afternoon, she had left her thoughts about the privacy of the soul in order to attend to preparations for that party. Besides reflecting on life Clarissa makes a positive contribution to it by occupying herself with the trivial and often irksome details involved in the day-to-day organizing of life. She is caught up in the 'ebb and flow' of life at both the surface of existence and in the deep regions below the surface.

Peter Walsh's story begins and ends with Clarissa Dalloway. Clarissa thinks of him on the first page of the novel, and the novel concludes with his awareness of her. His consciousness is also fully explored by Virginia Woolf, and she does this, in the main, by detecting the 'rhythmic order' underlying his thought and action. The rhythms of his fluctuating moods of elation and despondency are heard with insistence throughout the novel, and it is not surprising to find that many of the rhythmic progressions of his thoughts and feelings stem from his perplexity at, and analysis of, his relationship to Clarissa. Images very similar to the set of images that conveys Clarissa's fluctuating thoughts and feelings register and trace the rhythmic order of his life.

The first of Peter Walsh's rhythms as he leaves Dean's Yard is conditioned by what he had felt during his visit to Clarissa. He rushes from her house repeating her parting words rhythmically to himself: 'Remember my party, remember my party...'(54). As he strides along he keeps in step with the sound of Big Ben striking the half-hour (11.30 a.m.), and his words are uttered in tune also with the sound of Big Ben. Virginia Woolf draws significance out of Clarissa's ordinary injunction to remember her party. Meaning, it has already been noted, accrues to the concept of 'the party' as the novel progresses. Symbolically, it stands for life as it is generated by the rituals of an occasion that brings people together, that requires dressing up, and imposes a certain constraint in speech and behaviour. For Peter Walsh, however, it stands for Clarissa's choice of Richard Dalloway rather than himself, because it is Richard, the conventional man, the Conservative M.P., who provides Clarissa with her elegant drawing-room and entry into the Mayfair and Westminster world (the social and political worlds) from which most of her guests are drawn. Peter Walsh resents Richard Dalloway's influence on Clarissa, feeling not only that he has brought out one of the worst aspects of her character, her snobbishness, but also that Clarissa has failed to develop her own personality sufficiently in that she has been content to reflect, or shelter behind, that of her husband. She herself thinks this earlier in the day when she has the sense that she is invisible, only one of the anonymous crowd walking up Bond Street, 'this being Mrs. Dalloway; not even Clarissa any more; this being Mrs. Richard Dalloway'(13). And in his walk away from Regent's Park later in the day, Peter Walsh reflects that

> With twice his [Richard Dalloway's] wits, she had to see things through his eyes – one of the tragedies of married life... These parties, for example, were all for him, or for her idea of him....

(86)

Clarissa and her party-giving, Clarissa as the perfect hostess, then, is what Clarissa has become as a consequence of her not marrying Peter Walsh, and with his rhythmical repetition of the phrase 'remember my party' he is forcing that realization home to himself. He goes on teasing out in an irritated way the manner in which Clarissa has frittered her life away. And like a dog worrying at a bone he reiterates his disapproval in a repeated reference to her parties: 'Oh these parties? he thought; Clarissa's parties. Why does she give these parties? he thought'(54).

As Peter Walsh goes on criticizing Clarissa he weighs against her frivolous existence his own more real and richer life. But then as his emotion subsides he looks more honestly at himself and his own life. He looks symbolically into 'the glassy depths' and admits with shame and anguish his own failure and folly. More significantly, he reveals in three words why he is so angry at Clarissa: 'He stood there thinking, Clarissa refused me'(55).

THE RHYTHMIC ORDER OF *MRS. DALLOWAY*

Initiating this moment of stillness and truth is a 'flapping' movement -- 'Time flaps on the mast'(55) – which is an unobtrusive indicator of the sea symbolism, and more specifically of its ebb and flow of movement. Clarissa had, in the course of his visit to her, evoked their past associatively by reference to that same movement: 'Do you remember ... how the blinds used to flap at Bourton?'(47). This recalls to the reader the novel's first reference to Bourton and the past in which Clarissa remembered that the air at Bourton was 'like the flap of a wave'(5). It is picked up again at the party when the curtains blow out and are sucked back, or are beaten back, by one of the guests. The flap of the blinds or curtains, in other words, is being linked through the wave reference to the controlling imagery of the sea.

As Peter Walsh walks on, and as his emotion subsides, the rhythm of his stride slows down to keep pace, this time, with the sound of St Margaret's striking the half-hour. The rhythm is pleasing: its sound 'glides into the recesses of the heart' as Clarissa had done in his youth. But then as that sound dies away, it languishes, it makes him think of the present rather than the past, of death and old age rather than youth and vitality. The middle-aged Peter Walsh is feeling his years, and he has detected signs of ageing in Clarissa. But he puts these darker thoughts out of his mind, and one of his ways of doing this is by finding, and adapting his thoughts to, a new rhythm. He finds his rhythm by quickening his step, and his thoughts become positive as they pick up the more vigorous rhythm of his walk:

> No! No! he cried. She is not dead! I am not old, he cried, and marched up Whitehall, as if there rolled down to him, vigorous, unending, his future.
>
> (56)

There is then another external rhythm which causes Peter Walsh to draw his thoughts away from his preoccupation with Clarissa. That rhythm has two aspects to it. There is the 'patter like the patter of leaves in a wood'(57), but behind this there comes a more disturbing sound that exerts a certain control over his mind: 'a rustling, regular thudding sound ... drummed his thoughts, strict in step, up Whitehall, without his doing'(57). It is significant, however, that it is Peter Walsh's mind and not his feet that keep in step with the weedy boys in uniform. Having told himself that he is not old he is, ironically, unable to keep up with the marching column, and after it has passed him he has to pause on the pavement. There he analyses the rhythm of the marching boys and elicits its significance.

They walk like clockwork. He respects the 'marble stare' of their disciplined thought and feeling that is expressed symbolically in the rhythm of their steady march 'as if one will worked legs and arms uniformly'(57). Noting their discipline, he turns back to himself to make a comparison. He himself has always lacked discipline in his personal life (he was sent down from Oxford, is a womanizer, and has drifted from job to job). Steadiness is something that he, unlike the dedicated youngsters, is temperamentally incapable of attaining. But as he probes further into what their discipline implies, he discovers that the splendid rhythm of its uniformity contains a destructive element in that it stems from, and requires, a denial of life: life has been drugged 'into a stiff yet staring corpse by discipline'(57). By implication, then, he is closer to life than he could ever have been if he had disciplined his life after the manner of these young soldiers. This instance illustrates well how Virginia Woolf often expresses her thought or argument through the concrete rather than in an abstract form. As the image of the marching column is turned round, is explored and developed, Peter Walsh expresses his argument about discipline which then turns into a rationalization of his own inadequacy and indiscipline. At this point he savours the freedom of his own life. His reflection on that freedom allows an easy transition to the next image.

His freedom stems, in the immediate present, from his having escaped from the usual constraints of his normal daily life, and from the fact that nobody, apart from Clarissa, knows that he is back in England. What particularly delights him is the sense of anonymity in standing unknown in Trafalgar Square in the middle of the morning. He brings together the fact of his being there, his having just

THE RHYTHMIC ORDER OF *MRS. DALLOWAY*

travelled by sea from India, and the feeling of the smallness of England into a condensed image which is endowed with a mythic quality in the reduction of specific place to the general and elemental, as in '... and the earth, after the voyage, still seemed an island to him'.

In this private island space of his own mind, in the bustling centre of London, Peter Walsh begins to indulge his new-found freedom extravagantly as he walks off in pursuit of an unknown young woman. His step, as he follows her, contrasts with that of the disciplined youths, as it takes on the jaunty rhythms of his reckless thoughts. But as the young woman reaches her destination and evades him, the rhythm of Clarissa's voice calling 'Remember my party, Remember my party, sang in his ears'(60): the sound that had set his pace as he had walked away from Westminster to Great Portland Street with its shifting rhythms began and ended with the rhythm that asserts the pull of the unattainable woman in his life, Clarissa Dalloway.

Accepting that his escapade is over, Peter Walsh walks away with, this time, a new down-to-earth rhythm in his step. Again the rhythm of his walk reflects the new steadiness of his thoughts as he plans to put in the time before his appointment at Lincoln's Inn by visiting Regent's Park: 'His boots on the pavement struck out "no matter"; for it was early, still very early'(61). With this rhythm he exchanges the excitement of his own mind, his fantasy, for the excitement and vitality of the London scene around him. As he becomes absorbed in this life, its variety, he becomes aware of its rhythm which is one that suggests that it has a life of its own: 'Like the pulse of a perfect heart, life struck straight through the streets'(61). In Regent's Park the pulsating city sounds become distanced; they mingle with the sounds of the park to lull him to sleep:

A great brush swept smooth across his mind, sweeping
across it moving branches, children's voices, the shuffle of
feet, and people passing, and humming traffic, rising and
falling traffic. Down, down he sank into the plumes and
feathers of sleep, sank, and was muffled over.

(63)

VIRGINIA WOOLF AND THE POETRY OF FICTION

As he drifts into sleep the 'rhythmic order' of his consciousness modulates to be caught up in the novel's all-pervading sea imagery, because the city sounds 'rising and falling' are, in fact, the rhythm of the waves. And Peter Walsh 'sinks' into sleep.

The sea and its rhythmic movement pervades Peter Walsh's sleep. The womanly forms in his dream 'murmur in his ear like sirens lolloping away on the sea green waves', or they 'rise to the surface like pale faces which fishermen flounder through floods to embrace'. These visions 'ceaselessly float up' and the figure that offers him 'compassion, comprehension, absolution' rises 'from the troubled sea'(64). This world of watery visions is the world of the unconscious released in sleep through dreams. Central to the visions has been an archetypal woman form. In his waking life his major preoccupation is with two particular women, Daisy and Clarissa. They are embodied in strange forms in sleep. Water is the element that contains and, by association, expresses both. As he wakes he remembers scene after scene at Bourton, and then rouses himself to take notice of his surroundings again. After leaving Regent's Park he takes a taxi for Lincoln's Inn.

There are two more sections of Peter Walsh's walk through London. The one covers his return to his Bloomsbury Hotel where he dresses for dinner and decides to go to Clarissa's house in Westminster. It is, during these walks, essentially the sea imagery with its rhythmic ebb and flow that expresses both his introspection and his response to what is going on around him. There is, however, one moment in particular in which the inner and the outer worlds come together for Peter Walsh, and the instance resembles the moment described by Virginia Woolf in A Room of One's Own. Absorbed by his own thoughts and feeling the weight of the day upon him, 'the drip, drip of one impression after another'(167), he is brought out of himself by the sound of the light high bell of an ambulance rushing past him on its way to some hospital. On first hearing the sound he thinks of the power of the organization that can handle emergencies so efficiently. He sees it, in other words, as but one instance of the achievement of the British social structure, and even more generally as 'a triumph of civilisation'(166). Many of his reactions to what he sees on this

78

THE RHYTHMIC ORDER OF *MRS. DALLOWAY*

June day are conditioned by seeing everything anew after an absence of five years, and also in noting what has altered during those five years. The ambulance and its unknown occupant (it is presumably Septimus Warren Smith) stir Peter Walsh's imagination and he is moved by his own imaginings. As the sound of the bell dies away he turns inwards to note how his emotional and fanciful nature – 'his susceptibility' – has been his undoing. It is at this point that things 'come together' for him. Being exhausted by the day and its happenings, and feeling the proximity of life and death, he experiences a moment of intense awareness and it is associated with the precise spot he is standing at, and with the ambulance as it passes that place. His experience is, in other words, expressed by the way in which something outside himself connects with something within. The rhythm of the ambulance bell cuts across his private thoughts, and as the ambulance turns the corner he reflects that life is full of turns and corners. The thought and the physical correlative connect. To reinforce even further this moment of being intensely alive, or of being close to life, Virginia Woolf describes the experience again, but this time in terms of sea imagery:

> It was as if he were sucked up to some very high roof by that rush of emotion, and the rest of him, like a white shell-sprinkled beach, left bare.
>
> (167)

Virginia Woolf here indicates the mystical nature of Peter Walsh's experience, in that he is so taken out of himself that his innermost being is removed to a plane remote from his physical nature.

The intensity of this experience recalls to Peter Walsh Clarissa's 'transcendental theory' by which she believed that a part of one, the unseen part, might survive after death, and that 'she felt herself everywhere.... She waved her hand going up Shaftesbury Avenue. She was all that'(168). He has, in fact, just felt the kind of thing she had tried to explain to him nearly thirty years ago. Increasingly, and particularly in his walk back to Westminster, he becomes more intensely aware of the life of 'all that' that is around him. Behind Clarissa's theory, and evidenced in her walk to Bond Street, was the

79

VIRGINIA WOOLF AND THE POETRY OF FICTION

perception that 'life' was, besides being within one, also all around one, 'In people's eyes, in the swing, tramp, and trudge; in the bellow and the uproar...'(6). And she felt that 'on the ebb and flow of things, here, one survived'(11). Clarissa's feelings about life are ambiguous; the life that is delightful and exhilarating can also be fraught with danger and menace. She expresses the ambiguity of her feelings through straightforward images of the sea: she is alternately 'out, far out at sea and alone', and afloat 'on the ebb and flow of things'(11). Peter Walsh's apprehension of the 'ebb and flow' of the life around him is similar to Clarissa's, but his thoughts are never quite as dark as hers.

In the whole of his walk to Dean's Yard, Peter Walsh is buoyed up on that 'ebb and flow' as the whole of his experience is one of excitement and exhilaration. Returning to the hotel it had been, mostly, the 'privacy of the soul' that had preoccupied him, and it was from within that 'privacy' that his deepest feelings had sprung. In setting out for the party he consciously leaves the 'privacy of the soul', the inner world of his introspection, and the image that indicates his return to the surface life of what is going on around him is a playful one. It reflects his lighter mood. It is, however, the tone only that is light, for in one of his pessimistic moods the same images could express his despair.

> For this is the truth about our soul, he thought, our self, who fish-like inhabits deep seas and plies among obscurities threading her way between the boles of giant weeds, over sun-flickered spaces and on and on into gloom, cold, deep, inscrutable; suddenly she shoots to the surface and sports on the wind-wrinkled waves....
>
> (177)

Peter Walsh 'shoots' suddenly to the 'surface', and the world around him reflects his buoyancy of spirit. His journey to Dean's Yard is one of delight as he 'sports on the wind-wrinkled waves'.

Old Miss Parry, Clarissa's aunt, suddenly comes into his mind as he compares the present with the past. She is a landmark of his private life in that she belonged to Bourton: he remembered standing by her chair and how she had

THE RHYTHMIC ORDER OF *MRS. DALLOWAY*

guessed at his torment. But she is a landmark of another sort in that she belonged to an age that has now passed. She belongs to 'life', in other words, both in its individual and personal aspect, and also in its wider span of history. Peter Walsh pays tribute to her importance in life by the imagery through which he describes her:

> She ... would always stand up on the horizon, stone-white, eminent, like a lighthouse marking some past stage on this adventurous, long, long voyage ... this interminable life.
>
> (179)

As he makes his way through London, observing the scene, the whole populace seems to him to be very much alive, to be caught up in the ebb and flow of the city's vitality. He expresses this fancifully:

> it seemed as if the whole of London were embarking in little boats moored to the bank, tossing on the waters, as if the whole place were floating off in carnival.
>
> (180)

Peter Walsh's journey ends at Clarissa's house. The excitement and sense of life that has borne him on has, though he does not realize it, to do with her. The ebb and flow of the London streets has carried him to 'the lightened house' – the name 'Clarissa' suggests brightness. In that house he sees her as a vibrant creature in her own element, as a mermaid figure in her sea-green dress 'lolloping on the waves and braiding her tresses'. Essentially, however, he brings himself to acknowledge her power for life, her gift 'to be; to exist'(191). This is where his journey, expressed by the rhythmic order of the sea, has ultimately brought him.

The negative side of the life that both Peter Walsh and Clarissa endeavour to master dominates the broken personality of Septimus Warren Smith. The 'rhythmic order' of the sea asserts to what extent he is overwhelmed by life, and also draws attention to the rare moments in which he 'surfaces' from the painful depths of his private hell. In the Regent's Park episodes of the novel the process of drifting between the world of total madness and the borderline between sanity and insanity is revealed most cogently through imagery. The rough

81

VIRGINIA WOOLF AND THE POETRY OF FICTION

grasshopperlike voice of the nursemaid in the park, for instance, which he finds pleasant, sends 'waves of sound which, concussing, broke'(25), running up into his brain. There are all around him 'waves' of both sound and movement. The voice quickens the trees into life until their rhythmic waving, which seems to suggest an excess of life, terrifies Septimus. The rhythmic movement of the trees together with the pattern of colour that the movement creates is likened to the movement of the sea.

> the excitement of the elm trees rising and falling, rising and
> falling with all their leaves alight and the colour thinning
> and thickening from blue to the green of a hollow wave, like
> plumes on horses' heads, feathers of ladies', so proudly they
> rose and fell, so superbly, would have sent him mad.
>
> (26)

The sparrows 'fluttering, rising, and falling in jagged fountains' become part of the rhythmic pattern. But the initial feeling of delight in the rhythmic beauty of the sights and sounds around him in the park turns to fear and despair as Septimus thinks that the intensity will drive him mad.

As Septimus gradually becomes locked inside his own hallucinating mind he imagines himself to be 'high on his rock, like a drowned sailor on a rock'(77). In this mental position he lives out a fantasy of what has happened to him, and then using the same terms that control his fantasy he observes himself returning to the surface world of normality, of where he is:

> I leant over the edge of the boat and fell down, he thought.
> I went under the sea. I have been dead, and yet am now
> alive, but let me rest still, he begged (he was talking to
> himself again - it was awful, awful!); and as, before waking,
> the voices of birds and the sound of wheels chime and
> chatter in a queer harmony, grow louder and louder, and
> the sleeper feels himself drawing to the shores of life, so he
> felt himself drawing towards life, the sun growing hotter,
> cries sounding louder, something tremendous about to
> happen.

THE RHYTHMIC ORDER OF *MRS. DALLOWAY*

... He strained; he pushed; he looked; he saw Regent's Park before him.

(77)

Here there is an interplay between related images expressing different realities (sleep and death) but all are controlled by the ideas implicit in the rhythmic movement of rising and falling, of going below the surface and returning to it, and are associated, again, with the sea as an archetypal image of life. Septimus feels alternately aloof from life or submerged by it, and these feelings, together with his moments of being conscious of the real world outside his head, are all related to the ebb and flow of life that bears Clarissa Dalloway and Peter Walsh through this June day in London, and to the wider ebb and flow movement of the novel as a whole in which all the characters are caught up in some way.

Lady Bradshaw, for instance, 'is wedged on a calm ocean'. She has lost her free spirit. And Virginia Woolf notes with compassion the way in which marriage to her coercive husband has diminished her life:

Fifteen years ago she had gone under ... there had been no scene, no snap; only the slow sinking, water-logged, of her will into his.

(111)

Clarissa Dalloway, on the other hand, knowing only the social or surface aspect of her personality, which is neither pleasant nor attractive, perceives that lady as someone 'balancing like a sea-lion at the edge of its tank, barking for invitations, Duchesses, the typical successful man's wife...'(200).

The society world has its own ebb and flow movement, and it is felt through all its levels. Hugh Whitbread, for instance, has been 'afloat on the cream of English society for fifty-five years'(114) whereas Peter Walsh, less socially successful, has 'come back, battered, unsuccessful, to their secure shores'(119). Doris Kilman's bitterness and grudge against life is in part due to her exclusion, except in a subservient role, from that world. Physically ungainly and socially gauche, she is described as 'an unwieldy battleship' as she makes her way through the Army and Navy Stores. But her pain at being unable to overcome

VIRGINIA WOOLF AND THE POETRY OF FICTION

her nature, and also in finding life in general overwhelming, is linked symbolically with the person she most resents and who causes her to feel that pain most intensely, Clarissa Dalloway. The link is made through the same image of the waves bound up with the striking of the clock. As it brings Clarissa a 'lap full of odds and ends' – 'all sorts of little things came flooding and lapping and dancing in on the wake of that solemn stroke' – it, at the same time, drenches Miss Kilman in her own anguish:

> Volubly, troublously, the late clock sounded, coming in on the wake of Big Ben, with its lap full of trifles. Beaten up, broken up by the assault of carriages, the brutality of vans ... the last relics of this lap full of odds and ends seemed to break, like the spray of an exhausted wave, upon the body of Miss Kilman standing still in the street for a moment to mutter 'It is the flesh.'
>
> (141)

Elizabeth's 'beautiful body in the fawn-coloured coat' contrasts with her tutor's clumsy and unlovely body, and in contrast, too, to the battleship image her elegant form makes her 'like the figure-head of a ship' as she 'sails' up the Strand on the top of an omnibus.

The ebb and flow movement of the waves is used playfully by Virginia Woolf to describe the rituals of service that cushion Lady Bruton against life. When Hugh Whitbread asks her for an address

> there was at once a ripple in the grey tide of service which washed round Lady Bruton day in, day out, collecting, intercepting, enveloping her in a fine tissue which broke concussions, mitigated interruptions, and spread round the house in Brook Street a fine net where things lodged and were picked out accurately, instantly by grey-haired Perkins....
>
> (119)

There is an interesting moment in the course of the day, in which in an almost literal sense the rhythm of time is interlocked symbolically with the controlling forces of the sea. This occurs when Richard Dalloway, feeling torpid with the

84

THE RHYTHMIC ORDER OF *MRS. DALLOWAY*

combination of the heat and a substantial lunch, senses, as he pauses with Hugh Whitbread at the corner of Conduit Street, that

> Contrary winds buffeted at the street corner. They looked in at a shop window; they did not wish to buy or to talk but to part, only with contrary winds buffeting the street corner, with some sort of lapse in the tides of the body, two forces meeting in a swirl, morning and afternoon, they paused.
>
> (124)

And as he goes into the jeweller's shop with Hugh he develops, through a certain amount of repetition, his image of being buffeted by life: 'But there are tides in the body. Morning meets afternoon.' And all that has occupied his mind in the last hour or so – Lady Bruton's great-grandfather and America – is borne off 'like a frail shallop on deep, deep floods'(125) until it finally sinks.

The ebb and flow of life in which the individual is caught up and which bears him on is the 'force in things' that Virginia Woolf detects behind the ordinary scenes and events of her fiction, and which she registers in the 'rhythmic order'. That 'rhythmic order' finds its resolution at the party in which the private and the public are 'assembled' in Clarissa's drawing-room.

The party has a low-key beginning, an external climax (Clarissa's walk in her drawing-room with the Prime Minister), the psychological climax of her vicariously sharing in the death of Septimus Warren Smith, and an emotional climax in her silent apotheosis at the end.

As the guests arrive Clarissa greets each effusively with the formula: 'How delightful to see you!'(184). Peter Walsh reacts to the repeated empty words with anger and resentment, regretting that he had bothered to come to the party. Clarissa interprets the irritation she senses in his manner as a criticism of herself and at once feels despondent. One glimpse of Peter's disapproving countenance is, in other words, sufficient to alter the whole cast of her mind, and so to condition her emotional outlook. This is because she knows it to stem from his disapproval of something fundamental in her – her snobbery and the frivolity of her life. His glance so dampens

VIRGINIA WOOLF AND THE POETRY OF FICTION

her spirits that she believes her party to be a failure: the collection of people around her are not forming a whole; they are, instead, merely 'people wandering aimlessly'(184). What then brings the party haphazardly to life is the movement of the curtain, a movement that is essentially an 'ebb and flow' movement. 'Gently the yellow curtain with the birds of Paradise blew out ... right out, then sucked back'(185). So the isolated, separate people standing about in the Dalloway drawing-room become the party, they begin to be 'assembled'. The life that is figured in the movement of the curtain has taken over so that the fragments (isolated individuals) begin to cohere. Then, as Clarissa notices a more contented Peter Walsh walking off with her husband, and sees at the same time the curtain blowing out again and the way in which a guest beats it back, she decides that everything will be all right. 'So it wasn't a failure after all! it was going to be all right now – her party. It had begun. It had started. But it was still touch and go'(187). As Clarissa gently nurtures the thing she is bringing to life, the visible world of the party, and also, at the same time, the inner reality of something 'assembled', she takes note of the price she has to pay for the thing she creates: She 'felt herself a stake driven in at the top of her stairs. Every time she gave a party she had this feeling of being something not herself...'(187). Even so, as she formally receives each guest, she has not totally relinquished her inner life. She reflects on the paradox that at a social occasion like this party, at which people act out roles, wear special clothes, and so on, it is nevertheless possible 'to say things you couldn't say anyhow else, things that needed an effort; possible to go much deeper'(188). She distinguishes by implication in what she says to herself ('But not for her; not yet anyhow') that she is fully aware that at the moment it is only the surface of her self that is engaged in the party, with people, though it is possible on such a formal occasion to reach to a more profound level of awareness and communication. She begins to do this when Sally Seton arrives. In the spontaneous delight of seeing her old friend again the party is actually 'assembled'– the room full of people takes on for Clarissa a significance that transcends its actuality: '... and Clarissa turned, with Sally's hand in hers, and saw her rooms full, heard the roar of voices, saw the candlesticks, the blowing

86

THE RHYTHMIC ORDER OF *MRS. DALLOWAY*

curtains, and the roses which Richard had given her'(188). A whole has, in fact, been fashioned out of the various elements of Clarissa's life: her past, her husband's affection (she notices the roses), her social success, and the blowing curtains which, symbolically, set the life of the party flowing. It is now possible for her to 'go much deeper'. The party has come to life and she is of it.

The next stage in the progression follows as the Prime Minister is announced and Clarissa escorts him into her drawing-room. Although no one is in any doubt about the dullness of the human being below the fine trappings of his dress (he is 'all rigged up in gold lace'), they are moved by what he stands for in much the same way that the crowds in Piccadilly had been impressed by the Prime Minister's car as it made its slow progress through the morning traffic. The Prime Minister represents their life, English society. The guests at the Dalloway party are moved by a sense of patriotism. At this point, in other words, a corporate reality is experienced through the medium of a very ordinary person and an occasion of no real significance in itself. This is expressed through the wave image: 'Old Lady Bruton swam up ... a sort of stir and rustle rippled through every one openly: the Prime Minister!'(189).

At this level, too, Clarissa is 'afloat' at her party: symbolically 'lolloping on the waves' she is 'a creature floating in its element'(191). This is her social achievement. Clarissa judges, however, that this is but a 'hollow' triumph. For her the reality at the centre of the party is her own essential life that is made up of her husband and her daughter and her close friends from the past – Sally Seton and Peter Walsh. This is one of those moments in which it has been possible for Clarissa to 'go much deeper' as she realizes that it is her life of personal relationships and not the 'intoxication of the moment' that is of central importance in her life.

It is Lady Bradshaw's mentioning Septimus Warren Smith's suicide that leads to the second climax of the party. As death intrudes in this way into her party, into her life, Clarissa responds by withdrawing into the 'little room' of her self. So life and death come together at the party; death momentarily disrupts life and as it does so 'the party's splendour fell to the floor'(202). Clarissa, imagining the actual physicality of the

VIRGINIA WOOLF AND THE POETRY OF FICTION

suicide, compares with it something that she herself had done. He had thrown himself from a window; she had thrown a shilling into the Serpentine. And she asks if he had 'plunged holding his treasure'.

The treasure is the thing that matters in life ('a thing ... obscured in her own life, let drop every day in corruption, lies, chatter'(202)), the reality that is perceived for only an instant and which seems always to be escaping. The 'chatter and lies' surround Clarissa at the party, but also at the party she finds the reality embedded in it. In asking her question about Septimus she juxtaposes with it a cryptic statement about herself:

> But this young man who had killed himself – had he
> plunged holding his treasure? 'If it were now to die, 'twere
> now to be most happy,' she had said to herself once, coming
> down, in white.

(202–3)

'Plunging' is a word used by Virginia Woolf in this novel to imply the throwing of oneself into life: 'What a lark! What a plunge!'(5). With these words, on the opening page of the novel, Clarissa 'plunges' metaphorically into the June day in a way similar to the way in which she had, as a young girl, 'plunged' into the fresh air at Bourton that was like 'the flap of a wave'. So the word 'plunge' which she uses to describe Septimus's jump from the window is one of the cluster of words, like both 'flap' and 'wave', that links back to the controlling symbolism of the sea and its rhythmic evocation of life. But the two sentences are, in addition, a fine example of Virginia Woolf's extremely condensed writing in which layers of meaning can be peeled away from an allusion which draws together into itself instances and people from other sections of the novel.

Othello's words 'If it were now to die' had come into Clarissa's mind earlier in the day and had been connected with her feelings for Sally Seton. When she had felt despondent after her return from Bond Street Clarissa had gone upstairs 'as if she had left a party'(35), as if, that is, life was being denied her. In her attic bedroom she recalls the intensity of her feeling for Sally, and in doing so relives the actual

88

THE RHYTHMIC ORDER OF *MRS. DALLOWAY*

occasion, remembering where she was, her thoughts, and what she was wearing. She remembers that her feelings were those of Othello: '... and going downstairs, and feeling as she crossed the hall "if it were now to die 'twere now to be most happy." ' (39), and that the reason she was so excited was 'all because she was coming down to dinner in a white frock to meet Sally Seton' (39). Othello's words, the white frock, descending the staircase, belong, then, to the time of her life when she had been most happy, felt most strongly, and had 'plunged' into the air of Bourton and into life and what life was offering to her. That was also when she had refused Peter Walsh and had decided to marry Richard Dalloway.

Significantly, therefore, another instance in the novel is linked associatively with Clarissa's cryptic response to hearing about Septimus's death. It is the curious moment of terror that Peter Walsh has when he momentarily thinks that Clarissa is dead. As he allows the painful memory of her refusal to marry him to control his thoughts, the occasion on which that happened forces itself so strongly upon his consciousness that he visualizes it to himself again in his mind. What he sees is Clarissa 'coming downstairs on the stroke of the hour in white' (56). At this moment, as the stroke of St Margaret's dies away, Peter Walsh undergoes a strange psychological experience that is very like the reaction of Clarissa on hearing of the death of the shell-shocked Septimus. It brings death into his life as the suicide does into Clarissa's. In his strange imagination Clarissa dies – something in him died when she refused him. He is intensely aware of death in the midst of this June day in the streets of London. Clarissa's seeming death had taken place in her drawing-room, as Septimus's real death had also, in a sense, been brought into her drawing-room.

> and the sudden loudness of the final stroke tolled for death that surprised in the midst of life, Clarissa falling where she stood, in her drawing-room.
>
> (56)

Peter Walsh then denies this death and faces life as it is: 'No! No! he cried. She is not dead! I am not old, he cried, and marched up Whitehall' (56). Similarly Clarissa, having vicariously experienced Septimus's death, turns back to life,

89

though she admits its terror – 'Then ... there was the terror; an overwhelming incapacity, one's parents giving it into one's hands, this life, to be lived to the end...' (203). She goes back to the drawing-room to find her life as it is embedded symbolically in the party: 'But she must go back. She must assemble. She must find Sally and Peter. And she came in from the little room' (205).

The party ends unfiguratively with a reality that has been expressed largely figuratively throughout the novel. Peter Walsh, sitting on a sofa with Sally Seton, is still looking for the woman he has sought throughout the day, first in his visit to Clarissa, second in fantasy as he had followed an unknown woman along the London streets, third and subconsciously in sleep in Regent's Park, and finally in returning to Clarissa's drawing-room at the end of the day with mixed feelings of elation and apprehension. At the party he finds an answer to his question:

> What is this terror? what is this ecstasy? he thought to himself. What is it that fills me with extraordinary excitement?
>
> It is Clarissa, he said.
>
> For there she was.

(213)

What the reader is left with at the end of the novel is the reality that has been explored figuratively through the 'rhythmic order' with which Virginia Woolf has invested the various scenes, reflections, and occurrences of the novel.

Chapter Five

TO THE LIGHTHOUSE: AN ELEGY

All that Virginia Woolf has been moving towards, all that has been, as it were, gathering force below the narrative surface of her two 'traditional' novels, *The Voyage Out* and *Night and Day*, or that has been investigated and in part denied in the authorial intrusions of her third novel, *Jacob's Room*, comes into its own to find satisfactory expression in the three novels of her middle period. They are generally considered to be her best works. In these novels, inner and outer, the factual and visionary, intellect and feeling, and other related dichotomies achieve a satisfying unity. Vision is expressed through form, and the verbal texture of the works explores and expresses that vision and reinforces the form. The 'rhythmic order' of *Mrs. Dalloway*, as we have seen, rises from and expresses the 'unity of consciousness'. There is, in other words, a unity at the level of the novel's verbal texture, and also an inner or deeper structure of implication and meaning. But the different layers are also unified. This kind of 'unity' is essentially 'poetic'.

It is not surprising, therefore, to discover that while still working on *Mrs. Dalloway* and at the same time turning her mind to the novel that is to follow it, Virginia Woolf reveals a new interest in poetry, and also a realization that the way in which she responds to the world around her, and at a more abstract and mystical level to a sense of the mystery of the universe, is essentially poetic. It is more especially from this layer of her mind and this kind of consciousness that *To the Lighthouse* was created.

The significance of the poetic both as a way of perceiving and also as a mode of expression is constantly referred to in

91

VIRGINIA WOOLF AND THE POETRY OF FICTION

her diary in the mid-1920s. She eventually formulated her thoughts on this subject in an essay ('The Narrow Bridge of Art') that was published in the same year as *To the Lighthouse*.

The incipient novel and a sense of the poetic are linked together as early as 1923: she writes that she is overcome by a general sense of the poetry of existence and that this is connected with the sea and St Ives (*AWD*: 56). A year later she records that she is immersed in poetry, reading, in particular, long poem (*AWD*: 65).

By the following year she is beginning to grapple with some of the problems related to her need to find an appropriate form for the complexity of what she experiences in, or perceives through, the workings of her poetic imagination. Having found the subject and theme of the book, for which she also has the title, she writes:

> But this theme may be sentimental; father and mother and child in the garden; the death; the sail to the Lighthouse. I think, though, that when I begin it I shall enrich it in all sorts of ways; thicken it; give it branches – roots which I do not perceive now. It might contain all characters boiled down; and childhood; and then this impersonal thing, which I'm dared to do by my friends, the flight of time and the consequent break of unity in my design. That passage (I conceive the book in 3 parts. 1.at the drawing room window; 2.seven years passed; 3.the voyage) interests me very much. A new problem like that breaks fresh ground in one's mind; prevents the regular ruts.
>
> (*AWD*: 80–1; 20 July 1925)

and

> The thing is I vacillate between a single and intense character of father; and a far wider slower book....
> I think I might do something in *To the Lighthouse*, to split up emotions more completely. I think I'm working in that direction.
>
> (*AWD*: 81; 30 July 1925)

All her thinking and theorizing, then, as she began to write *To the Lighthouse*, seems more appropriate to the writing of poetry

than to the writing of prose fiction. It is not surprising, therefore, that she thinks of *To the Lighthouse* as something other
than a novel: 'I have an idea that I will invent a new name for
my books to supplant "novel". A new —— by Virginia Woolf.
But what? Elegy?'(*AWD*: 80). 'Elegy' certainly suits the idea of
'a far wider slower book', and the tone of this novel is, in fact,
elegiac. Ultimately, however, Virginia Woolf's writing is poetic
because of the cast of the mind that produces it: hers is a
visionary, image-making, highly visual consciousness that is
only satisfied when what it perceives comes together to form a
whole, a unity that bears the weight of meaning.

Virginia Woolf's art is often referred to by critics as 'impressionistic'; and it is certainly through impressionistic fragments, as we have seen, that the life of Jacob Flanders was
pieced together and his 'room' built up. And it is in those
fragments that the 'poetry' of that novel mostly inheres. But
impressionism as a term fails to do justice to the three novels
of her central phase. Her art in these works is more characteristically post-impressionistic. Her experimentation here has
enabled her to achieve the kind of total coherence in the
expression of her vision that Roger Fry writes of in his account
of the Post-Impressionist painters who exhibited at the Grafton
Galleries in 1910:

> They do not seek to imitate form, but to create form; not to
> imitate life, but to find an equivalent for life. By that I mean
> that they wish to make images which by the clearness of
> their logical structure, and by the closely-knit unity of
> texture, shall appeal to our disinterested and contemplative
> imagination with something of the same vividness as the
> things of actual life appeal to our practical activities. In fact,
> they aim not at illusion but at reality.
>
> (*Vision and Design*: 239)

There is an obvious similarity, then, between Roger Fry's
ideas about painting and Virginia Woolf's about literature,
particularly as they are expressed in her essay 'The Narrow
Bridge of Art' in which she discusses the significance of fiction
that is poetic in quality. Her own novels are, of course, works
of art by virtue of the poetry in them. The thrust of her
argument in 'The Narrow Bridge of Art' is that the novel of

the future will be one that has many of the characteristics of poetry, and that such a novel is the most appropriate form in which to express the complexity of the modern consciousness. This kind of novel will

> give the relations of man to nature, to fate; his imagination; his dreams. But it will also give the sneer, the contrast, the question, the closeness and complexity of life. It will take the mould of that queer conglomeration of incongruous things – the modern mind.
>
> ('The Narrow Bridge of Art', *CE* II: 226)

She refers to *Tristram Shandy*, for instance, as a book in which one sees poetry changing naturally and easily into prose and prose into poetry. The designation 'novel' will no longer be adequate:

> We shall be forced to invent new names for the different books which masquerade under this one heading [novel].
>
> ('The Narrow Bridge of Art', *CE* II: 224)

Roger Fry speaks of form and texture as the two means by which a work of art achieves unity. In the previous chapter I discussed the structure and texture of *Mrs.Dalloway* from specific examples, and in doing so a sense of the novel's quality of organic wholeness became more and more evident. It is, however, always easier to note qualities and aspects of 'texture' which give a work its more obvious 'poetic' quality than the point at which everything comes together to form a whole, or, in other words, the kind of formal originality that Roger Fry detected in Post-Impressionist art, and which is more difficult to pin down. When Virginia Woolf explores some of the ways in which the hypothetical novel of the future takes on the attributes of poetry she at the same time reveals some of the ways in which she herself is working towards new forms of fiction. One way is through her observation of the specifically 'modern' consciousness.

> The ordinary person is calmer, smoother, more self-contained than he used to be.
> ... He follows every thought careless where it may lead him. He discusses openly what used never to be mentioned even

privately. And this very freedom and curiosity are perhaps the cause of what appears to be his most marked characteristic – the strange way in which things that have no apparent connection are associated in his mind. Feelings which used to come single and separate do so no longer. Beauty is part ugliness; amusement part disgust; pleasure part pain. Emotions which used to enter the mind whole are now broken up on the threshold.

('The Narrow Bridge of Art', *CE* II: 222)

She is also enlarging the bounds of the 'psychological' novel to include 'impersonal' as well as personal relations. The new novel 'will give the relations of man to nature, to fate'. And as her perspective alters so also does the form of her fiction; it has to be constantly adapted to whatever it is she wishes to express. Glimpses of how she 'adapts' life to art are often to be found in her diary. One such instance in particular is very interesting because it shows how she might actually begin to bring together things that are not necessarily connected, and at the same time reveals how by her way of bringing things into a certain kind of relatedness experience begins to 'take the mould' of her mind.

First of all she records at length a visit she and her husband paid to Thomas Hardy. She gives a straightforward account of the visit, noting how he and his wife received them, what he looked like, and what they talked about. She also gives her impression of his personality, and also something of her own feelings when confronted by the great Victorian novelist who had known her father. At a later stage, when theorizing about the novel, she recalls this visit and imagines what she would do with it if she were to turn it into a story or a work of 'art'.

What I thought was this: if art is based on thought, what is the transmuting process? I was telling myself the story of our visit to the Hardys, and I began to compose it; that is to say to dwell on Mrs. Hardy leaning on the table, looking out apathetically, vaguely, and so would soon bring everything into harmony with that as the dominant theme. But the actual event was different.

(*AWD*: 95)

VIRGINIA WOOLF AND THE POETRY OF FICTION

In a similar kind of way Virginia Woolf adapts her own life to art; she submits her memory of her family to the same kind of 'transmuting process'. She tells herself the 'story' of her past. The bit she selects is her childhood, and, selectively again, the family summer holidays that were spent in a beautiful place that continued to haunt her for the rest of her life and which, at the level of image and symbol, forms part of the texture of her first six novels. As she told herself the 'story' of the Hardys she began to 'compose' it. As she composed she created a form: one strong feature was emphasized, and everything else was brought into harmony with it. Her analysis of her own procedure here has affinities with Roger Fry's analysis of Post-Impressionist paintings, and specific parallels with the way in which she creates the form of *To the Lighthouse*. The novel is made out of what can be easily summarized as follows: her father and mother, childhood and St Ives, the sail to the lighthouse and the universal themes of love and marriage, life and death. She starts to bring these ingredients into harmony through the image of her father in a boat:

> But the centre is father's character, sitting in a boat,
> reciting We perished, each alone, while he crushes a dying
> mackerel.

(AWD: 77)

In the completed novel, however, all is brought into harmony through a different image, that of her mother sitting in the window.

It is very significant that when Virginia Woolf had 'ordered' her visit to the Hardys into a composition she realized that the thing she had made was different from the original situation: 'But the actual event was different'. So too with the novel; her family and her past became altered as she shaped them into a work of fiction. *To the Lighthouse* is, in other words, an autobiographical novel, not autobiography. Lily Briscoe comparing what is on her canvas with the original in front of her is intrigued by the discrepancy between the real-life figure and the image she has made of her, '... thinking that she was unquestionably the loveliest of people (bowed over her book); the best perhaps; but also, different, and how different? she asked herself...' (79). Lily sees her composition in the same

TO THE LIGHTHOUSE: AN ELEGY

terms that Roger Fry uses, form and texture, though she expresses them metaphorically:

> She saw the colour burning on a framework of steel; the light of a butterfly's wing lying upon the arches of a cathedral.

(78)

Virginia Woolf has, in other words, placed in her novel an artist who acts as a kind of surrogate author since she is doing in painting what she herself is doing through language. Lily is a kind of metafictional presence in disguise. Like the metafictional narrator of *Jacob's Room* she tries to remain detached from what is before her in order to understand it and, in her case, turn it into a picture. But unlike the metafictional narrator she allows herself ultimately to enter the 'cave of mystery' so that at the end of the novel she acknowledges: 'I have had my vision'(320). It is this that enables her to draw the line in the centre of the canvas that brings everything into harmony, thus bringing the picture to completion.

The image of the woman reading to her child which moves Lily to try to capture its reality and express it in paint produces a similar intensity of feeling in William Bankes who stands beside her on the lawn looking towards that figure in the window. His love,

> like the love which mathematicians bear their symbols, or poets their phrases, was meant to be spread over the world and become part of the human gain. So it was indeed. The world by all means should have shared it, could Mr. Bankes have said why that woman pleased him so; why the sight of her reading a fairy tale to her boy had upon him precisely the same effect as the solution of a scientific problem, so that he rested in contemplation of it, and felt, as he felt when he had proved something absolute about the digestive system of plants, that barbarity was tamed, the reign of chaos subdued.

(77)

Lily interprets his response as a love that is 'distilled and filtered', or, in other words, as an aesthetic emotion which, according to Clive Bell, differs in kind from a purely human emotion since it is produced by a 'significant form' (*Art*: 25).

97

VIRGINIA WOOLF AND THE POETRY OF FICTION

But behind the image of the woman reading a fairy tale to her child lies the reality of the family she has created and sustains, and who depend on her for warmth and understanding. Behind the image, in other words, is Virginia Woolf's beautiful evocation of family life. That is what Mrs Ramsay has made out of her life, and its felt power draws to it unattached and lonely, though independent, individuals such as Lily Briscoe and William Bankes, Charles Tansley and Augustus Carmichael. Its magic is economically conveyed by such images as

The house seemed full of children sleeping and Mrs. Ramsay listening; of shaded lights and regular breathing.

(80)

Just as the image of Mrs Hardy leaning on the table summed up the reality of what Virginia Woolf had experienced on her visit to the Hardys, and was the structural feature that harmonized everything in the story of that visit, so Mrs Ramsay reading to her small son is the image that unifies Part I of the novel, and also, in a different kind of way, the novel as a whole. The novel is formed out of all that lies behind that image, and out of the response of all the other characters in the book to what it stands for. The surface of the book is, therefore, very slight. What is impressive is the exploration of layer upon layer below it, and the relation of facet to facet in the multi-perspectival exploration of the reality embodied in that image. And this kind of density of writing is, of course, more typical of poetry than fiction.

Lily, trying to understand Mrs Ramsay, and ultimately expressing through the medium of art the 'reality' of the novel, continually oscillates between resistance to the Ramsays' influence and an inability to do anything other than succumb to it. It is between those two positions that she negotiates the meaning inherent in the quality of life of a particular family in a particular house by the sea on a late September afternoon shortly before the outbreak of the Great War. As she stands on the lawn and looks towards Mrs Ramsay and the child, Mr Ramsay suddenly appears and moves, as it were, into the picture. From that new grouping of a man and a woman and a child emanates a powerful influence that touches those who

TO THE LIGHTHOUSE: AN ELEGY

come in contact with it. Others can experience vicariously through them a sense of life's potential wholeness. So Lily saw

> how life, from being made up of little separate incidents which one lived one by one, became curled and whole like a wave which bore one up with it and threw one down with it, there, with a dash on the beach.
>
> (76)

But then as she scrapes at the mounds of paint on her palette she tries to penetrate the mystery of what is enacted before her by using the analytic method of the metafictional narrator of *Jacob's Room.* Looking at Mrs Ramsay, she asks:

> How did she differ? What was the spirit in her, the essential thing, by which, had you found a glove in the corner of a sofa, you would have known it, from its twisted finger, hers indisputably?
>
> (79)

The whole episode of Lily Briscoe on the lawn is built out of the way in which she, in particular, explores what lies behind the mother and child image in terms of her own personal life and expectations. As she draws on past encounters with Mrs Ramsay, and on her observations of the family as a whole and their friends, her perceptions are recorded by the author. The radiance of Mr Bankes's countenance, for instance, as he gazes at Mrs Ramsay dispels Lily's reflections by drawing her into his feelings of reverent love for the mother reading a fairy story to her little boy:

> for nothing so solaced her, eased her of the perplexity of life, and miraculously raised its burdens, as this sublime power, this heavenly gift, and one would no more disturb it, while it lasted, than break up the shaft of sunlight lying level across the floor.
>
> (78)

It is often when she lets herself be taken over by her feelings for Mrs Ramsay that she, at the same time, has a visionary sense of her reality. This is conveyed to the reader by Virginia Woolf's presentation of Lily's consciousness. And it is because readers are given this kind of deeply felt awareness of Mrs

Ramsay, because they vicariously share another's profound perception of her, that they feel they know her. This is why she comes to life so vividly as her portrait is built up. It is through Lily's endless explorations of the reality behind the image that the author creates her most telling perspective of Mrs Ramsay.

By naming Part I of *To the Lighthouse* 'The Window' Virginia Woolf is indicating her angle of vision both for her presentation of Mrs Ramsay and also for structuring generally the substance of the novel. The first half of Part I is, in fact, entirely structured round the visual presentation of a woman reading a fairy story to her son together with reiterated reference to the child's wish to go to the lighthouse and the insistence of others, most significantly his father, that the weather will not be good enough to do so. The verbal exchange is worked out as follows, through the numbered sub-sections of Part I:

1

"Yes, of course, if it's fine to-morrow," said Mrs. Ramsay. "But you'll have to be up with the lark," she added.

(11)

"But," said his father, stopping in front of the drawing-room window, "it won't be fine."

(12)

"But it may be fine – I expect it will be fine," said Mrs. Ramsay....

(13)

"It's due west," said the atheist Tansley....

(14)

"Nonsense," said Mrs.Ramsay....

(15)

"There'll be no landing at the Lighthouse to-morrow," said Charles Tansley....

(17)

2

"No going to the Lighthouse, James," he [Tansley] said ....

(28)

TO THE LIGHTHOUSE: AN ELEGY

3

"Perhaps you will wake up and find the sun shining and the birds singing," she said....

(28)

5

"And even if it isn't fine to-morrow," said Mrs. Ramsay, raising her eyes to glance at William Bankes and Lily Briscoe as they passed, "it will be another day. And...."

(45)

6

There wasn't the slightest possible chance that they could go to the Lighthouse to-morrow, Mr. Ramsay snapped out irascibly.

How did he know? she asked. The wind often changed.

(53)

10

In a moment he would ask her, "Are we going to the Lighthouse?" And she would have to say, "No; not to-morrow; your father says not." ... and she was certain that he was thinking, we are not going to the Lighthouse to-morrow; and she thought, he will remember that all his life.

(98–9)

This reads with obvious monotony. Yet it is, apart from Lily's conversation with William Bankes, almost the entire verbal exchange for nearly a third of the novel. In reading the novel, however, one is almost unaware of it. It threads its way through the text as a leitmotiv does in a musical composition. But what gathering these remarks together brings home to one is the very restricted time-scale within which Virginia Woolf is working. The time covered is very short indeed, but the psychological experience undergone in it is vast. She is, in other words, exploiting in her art the discrepancy between 'clock' time and the Bergsonian sense of durational time.

Within that exchange and behind the image of the woman at the window reading to her small boy the rich substance of the novel grows and expands. There her visit to the village with Charles Tansley, in which he responds to her genuine interest and compassion and she realizes why he has such a chip on his shoulder and why, in part, he is such a bore, is recalled and re-enacted in her mind. There, too, the nature of

101

the relationship between her and her husband, and the relationship between father and child, in which the child resents the way in which his father comes between him and his mother, is revealed. Lily and William Bankes on the lawn reveal much about Mrs Ramsay.

All the felt life in the novel – the tensions between the intuitively conciliatory Mrs Ramsay and the ruthlessly intellectual Mr Ramsay who needs to be reassured by her that he lives at 'the heart of life'; Lily Briscoe working out her own life, overwhelmed by contact with the Ramsays, more especially by the power of Mrs Ramsay who wants her to marry, while at the same time trying to resist their collective influence so that she can make a way for herself that is different from theirs – is structured or 'brought into harmony' by the image of a woman reading a fairy tale to her child, and through the trite verbal exchange about the weather and going to the lighthouse. So too are such delightful touches as the large calm presence of Augustus Carmichael 'basking with his yellow cat's eyes ajar' or asking for another plate of soup, and the children creeping off to the fastnesses of their attics. The image is dismantled when James is taken off to bed. This is followed by a remarkable psychological analysis of the way in which Mrs Ramsay unifies her own fragmented inner life, restoring herself to wholeness, after being drained by the constant emotional demands that others make on her.

Mrs Ramsay needs moments of solitude in order to be the creative centre of the family. Such moments are restorative; they enable her first of all to be herself: 'a wedge-shaped core of darkness, something invisible to others'(99). Here she finds peace and stability.

> There was freedom, there was peace, there was, most
> welcome of all, a summoning together, a resting on a
> platform of stability.

(100)

At this deep level of being, below the level of personality, the self renews its life by bringing its scattered pieces together to form a whole. So Mrs Ramsay creates something whole out of her life as Lily does in her painting and Virginia Woolf does in her novel.

TO THE LIGHTHOUSE: AN ELEGY

The climax of the first part of the novel is the dinner party, but before that Mr and Mrs Ramsay take a stroll in the garden, and as they stop to watch two of their children throwing catches they are observed by Lily Briscoe and William Bankes who are also walking in the garden. Lily, therefore, views Mrs Ramsay from a different perspective. The focus changes because the pieces forming this new composition are placed in a different relation to each other.

So that is marriage, Lily thought, a man and a woman looking at a girl throwing a ball.

(114)

Lily absorbs meaning from what she sees visually. The new 'picture' represents emblematically, like a still from a film, the novel's central theme of love and marriage. It also conveys through an image the creative whole that Mr and Mrs Ramsay together have made of their lives through marriage. In this arrested view of them they assume symbolic proportions. They become archetypal man and woman, their particularity transcended to make them symbolically representative of man and woman united. But Mr and Mrs Ramsay are 'real' characters realistically presented despite the novel's poetic mode of narration. They are only momentarily viewed as symbols. This is emphasized as the narrator articulates Lily's experience:

Then, after an instant, the symbolical outline which transcended the real figures sank down again, and they became, as they met them, Mr. and Mrs. Ramsay watching the children throwing catches.

(115)

Much of the appeal of *To the Lighthouse* lies in the rich specificity of the real ordinary everyday life experience of these people; density and profundity are given to it through the poetic exploration of the general implications of the particular. Mr and Mrs Ramsay are viewed archetypally again, for instance, when a whole cluster of obvious female images (fountain and spray, rosy-flowered fruit tree) is attached to her, and obvious male images (beak of brass, arid scimitar) are attached to him. But they are never turned into mere symbolic representation.

The dinner party symbolizes Mrs Ramsay's ability to create

VIRGINIA WOOLF AND THE POETRY OF FICTION

something whole out of fragments; the fragments are isolated separate human beings who, to begin with, resist her wish to draw them out of their isolation. Her struggle to make the separate parts merge is conveyed through a cluster of images associated with the sea, thus linking that struggle with the journey to the lighthouse in the final part of the novel.

Mrs Ramsay, feeling outside the 'eddy' of life that should be bearing her along, begins to be drawn into it as she starts to feel sorry for William Bankes:

> she began all this business, as a sailor not without weariness sees the wind fill his sail and yet hardly wants to be off again and thinks how, had the ship sunk, he would have whirled round and round and found rest on the floor of the sea.
>
> (131)

Lily observes her 'as one follows a fading ship until the sails have sunk beneath the horizon'(132). When she revives, Lily thinks of her as a ship that turns with the sun on its sails (132). And when the 'ship' is set firmly on its course she decides, in a flash of inspiration, to move the tree to the middle of her picture. Mrs Ramsay's plea to her to be nice to Charles Tansley is a cry from someone who is drowning:

> I am drowning, my dear, in seas of fire. Unless you apply some balm to the anguish of this hour and say something nice to that young man there, life will run upon the rocks – indeed I hear the grating and the growling at this minute....
>
> (143)

It is the lighting of the candles that eventually enables the people round the table to merge; the light 'composes' them into a party round a table. Once this has happened, which means that Mrs Ramsay has reached a point of achievement and therefore of security, the occasion is viewed as one of escape from the dangers of the sea:

> here, inside the room, seemed to be order and dry land; there, outside, a reflection in which things wavered and vanished, waterily.
>
> (151)

TO THE LIGHTHOUSE: AN ELEGY

The party moves into a new phase with the arrival of Paul and Minta who have just become engaged; their joy spills over to touch the others.

As all now merge spontaneously and the atmosphere lightens, Mrs Ramsay relaxes in a position of security. She can, psychologically, leave them to get on with it and escape mentally for a moment to give herself up to her own feelings and reflections. She feels 'like a flag floated in an element of joy which filled every nerve of her body fully and sweetly'(162). It is the joy that comes from the satisfaction of successful creation. She has created a kind of living work of art by bringing these people into harmony with each other so that they form a whole which expresses something of the fundamental reality of her own life. It is she who holds her family together; on the outer rim of her sphere of influence her friends have been touched by her power and have responded to it.

There is an element of eternity (the moment 'partook ... of eternity') in her joy, and this brings her the same kind of peace and feeling of stability that she had experienced in her moment of solitude earlier in the afternoon. A connection between that moment of solitude and this moment of successful creation is made explicitly:

> there is a coherence in things, a stability; something, she meant, is immune from change, and shines out... in the face of the flowing, the fleeting, the spectral, like a ruby; so that again to-night she had the feeling she had had once to-day already, of peace, of rest. Of such moments, she thought, the thing is made that remains for ever after. This would remain.
>
> (163)

The dinner party must come to an end. But the reality of this moment, she feels, will endure in the hearts of others. It is this core of meaning that she tries to elicit from the evening when she pauses on her way upstairs to settle the younger children.

> She felt rather inclined just for a moment to stand still after all that chatter, and pick out one particular thing; the thing that mattered; to detach it; separate it off; clean it of all the

VIRGINIA WOOLF AND THE POETRY OF FICTION

emotions and odds and ends of things, and so hold it before her....

(174)

She rightly believes that after her death they will return 'to this night; this moon; this wind; this house; and to her too'(175). They do, though not all of them, ten years later, in Part III of the novel.

'The Window' is the richest of the novel's three parts, and its richness is created, as we have seen, through the poetic quality of the writing. The recurrence of images of the sea and the lighthouse, of light and darkness, and the symbolism of the journey, are all obvious poetic devices. But the essential poetic quality of the writing inheres in the density below, in particular, the central image of the mother reading a fairy story to her little boy. The writing has, in other words, many of the characteristics of Post-Impressionist painting. In Roger Fry's phrases, Virginia Woolf has created poetically 'an equivalent for life' through the structure of her images and in the novel's 'closely-knit unity of texture'. What the 'poetry' of this fiction achieves, however, is, paradoxically, an intensification of felt life. Vanessa Bell's response to her sister's evocation of her mother more than bears this out:

> In the first part of the book you have given a portrait of mother which is more like her than anything I could have conceived of as possible. You made me feel the extraordinary beauty of her character.... It was like meeting her again with oneself grown up and on equal terms.... You have given father too, I think as clearly, but perhaps.... that isn't quite so difficult. There is more to catch hold of.
>
> (Bell II: 127)

The central section of the novel is referred to by Virginia Woolf as

> the most difficult abstract piece of writing – I have to give an empty house, no people's characters, the passage of time, all eyeless and featureless with nothing to cling to....
>
> (AWD: 88)

106

TO THE LIGHTHOUSE: AN ELEGY

But what most significantly Virginia Woolf has given the reader 'to cling to' in this section is the vision of Mrs Ramsay; the spirit of the woman in the window haunts the bleak years of 'Time Passes'. The most important thing about the empty house is not that it is a completely neutral place, but that it is a haunted house, one that is full of associations and memories and meaning. This section is, then, a poetic interlude about the passage of time and an empty house. It is also about life and death, and love and war. Mrs Ramsay's death, as well as those of Prue and Andrew, is recorded in a detached factual manner: it is like reading of the death of a close friend in a newspaper. The narrative voice of this section is impersonal, the consciousness behind it authorial.

It opens with an elaborate virtuoso rhapsody on the theme of darkness which quickly establishes a multiplicity of implications ranging from the literal to the metaphysical. The lights are put out literally when the Ramsays and their friends retire to bed. The literal is then picked up and transposed to the metaphoric to suggest a force that is threatening and overwhelming:

So with the lamps all put out, the moon sunk, and a thin rain drumming on the roof a down-pouring of immense darkness began. Nothing, it seemed, could survive the flood....

(195–6)

The solemnity of the tone is then dispelled by humour as fantasy takes over in a passage that has similarities to Eliot's description of the fog in 'The Love Song of J. Alfred Prufrock':

the profusion of darkness which, creeping in at keyholes and crevices, stole round window blinds, came into bedrooms, swallowed up here a jug and basin, there a bowl of red and yellow dahlias, there the sharp edges and firm bulk of a chest of drawers.

(196)

The tone becomes increasingly whimsical as certain mysterious airs invade and explore the house. But ominously, as they leave, they give off a 'gust of lamentation'.

The next section of the interlude opens on a quite different

VIRGINIA WOOLF AND THE POETRY OF FICTION

note. The tone is authorial and cool. 'But what after all is one night?' Unobtrusively the narrative shifts into a personification of winter as a cruel Fate relentlessly dealing her dark cards:

> Night, however, succeeds to night. The winter holds a pack of them in store and deals them equally, evenly, with indefatigable fingers. They lengthen; they darken.
>
> (198)

This is followed by an allegorical representation of a wilful and irresponsible deity:

> But alas, divine goodness, twitching the cord, draws the curtain; it does not please him; he covers his treasures in a drench of hail, and so breaks them, so confuses them that *it seems impossible that* their calm should ever return or that *we should ever compose from their fragments a perfect whole* or read in the littered pieces the clear words of truth.
>
> (199) (my italics)

Here, in the italicized words, is the key to the novel, an authorial expression, though in a negative form, of what Mrs Ramsay has struggled for and what Lily goes on struggling with, succeeding only when she has finally completed her picture, and what Mr Ramsay accomplishes when he reaches the lighthouse. It is also, of course, what Virginia Woolf is trying to do through language in the novel. It rests on the belief that one can make the fragments cohere into a whole. 'Divine goodness' breaks up what he sees into fragments so that, despite the human spirit's urge to mend and heal, life at all levels, personal, domestic, national (the war), and, as if to keep in tune with this, the cosmic, reverts to chaos. The interlude on time embodies the dark moments of life, 'The Window' a moment of light, and 'The Lighthouse' a remembrance of that moment and a return to it symbolically in a movement towards the restoration of the light. The tripartite structure of the novel, therefore, with its symbolic pattern of alternating light and dark, reflects the shining of the lighthouse beam through the darkness. That beam is symbolically representative of Mrs Ramsay. From the security of her 'wedge-shaped core of darkness' she had looked out at the lighthouse and revealed that

TO THE LIGHTHOUSE: AN ELEGY

this thing, the long steady stroke, was her stroke. Often she found herself sitting and looking, sitting and looking, with her work in her hands until she became the thing she looked at – that light for example.

(100–1)

The lighthouse as the embodiment of that light is what Mr Ramsay must journey to, ten years later, in 'The Lighthouse'. When he reaches it Lily is able to complete her picture. At all levels of the novel, then, the fragments cohere to form a unity, a whole. That is possible in art but less possible in life, although the human condition characteristically aspires to it.

Virginia Woolf's interlude on the passing of time places the life of the Ramsays in a wider historical and metaphysical context, although this is expressed largely through the concrete presentation of a house slipping into decay but rescued at the last moment from total dissolution. Even though this section of the novel is essentially of an impersonal nature it is nevertheless shot through with detail that brings the reader back again and again to the life that was so closely observed and explored in 'The Window'. The house has always the feel of those who have lived there. Objects retain some mark of their departed owners or users. For instance:

What people had shed and left – a pair of shoes, a shooting cap, some faded skirts and coats in wardrobes – those alone kept the human shape and in the emptiness indicated how once they were filled and animated....

(200)

The felt life of the family is continually evoked, and there are indications throughout that the house had once been

a world hollowed out in which a figure turned, a hand flashed, the door opened, in came children rushing and tumbling....

(200)

The sense of absence central to this section is made the more poignant by reminders like this of the kind of presence the house had once held.

As Virginia Woolf builds up her account of how the fabric

VIRGINIA WOOLF AND THE POETRY OF FICTION

and structure of the house are undermined by invading forces of decay, she at the same time conveys how man's spirit is attacked by hostile forces that overwhelm him. She does this in a vision of violence and physical chaos that resembles in many ways the apocalyptic vision of Yeats's *Second Coming*.

> Listening ... from the upper rooms of the empty house only gigantic chaos streaked with lightning could have been heard tumbling and tossing, as the winds and waves disported themselves like the amorphous bulks of leviathans whose brows are pierced by no light of reason, and mounted one on top of another, and lunged and plunged in the darkness or the daylight (for night and day, month and year ran shapelessly together) in idiot games, until it seemed as if the universe were battling and tumbling, in brute confusion and wanton lust aimlessly by itself.

(208–9)

The vision of wanton lust, idiot games, and the darkness of unreason, is as devastating as Yeats's 'blood-dimmed tide' and 'rough beast' that 'slouches towards Bethlehem to be born'. But, unlike Yeats, Virginia Woolf believes that the flood will be stemmed, that there is the possibility of restoration, though things can never be exactly as they had been. Mrs McNab scrubs and cleans and the rats are caught, and as her task is completed 'some rusty laborious birth seemed to be taking place' (216).

Throughout the dark years of the house's decay a spirit is abroad searching for a point of rest and security at the heart of the turbulence in evidence all around. Virginia Woolf suggests through the piling up of image on image that despite the anguish of death and the destruction of war man can yet find some way of making sense of life, or, in Mrs Ramsay's terms, of bringing the scattered fragments of life into coherence. So the mystic wanderer on the shore has strange imaginings

> of flesh turned to atoms which drove before the wind, of stars flashing in their hearts, of cliff, sea, cloud, and sky brought purposely together to assemble outwardly the scattered parts of the vision within.

(204)

TO THE LIGHTHOUSE: AN ELEGY

Such dreams persist in the belief that 'good triumphs, happiness prevails, order rules'.

All the searches are, in fact, for the vision of reality glimpsed by Mrs Ramsay at the dinner party, and the kind of coherence she achieved in her own personal life. This is borne out by the allusive nature of the images in which the search is embodied. The mystic on the shore seeks 'some crystal of intensity' or something 'single, hard, bright, like a diamond in the sand, which would render the possessor secure'(205). At the dinner party Mrs Ramsay thought of her awareness of 'a coherence at the centre of things, a stability' as something changeless that shines out 'in the face of the flowing, the fleeting, the spectral, like a ruby'(163). At the darkest point of the dark years when Andrew is killed in the war the search seems futile; the vision of the seeker on the shore is shattered by the disturbing image of something both destructive and evil at the very heart of life:

> There was the silent apparition of an ashen-coloured ship
> for instance, come, gone; there was a purplish stain upon
> the bland surface of the sea as if something had boiled and
> bled, invisibly, beneath.
>
> (207)

This terrible image of the haemorrhaging away of life almost destroys man's faith in the possibility of survival, but just when the night is darkest, the house fallen almost beyond repair, the spirit of the mystic almost broken, the balance is gently shifted and the work of restoration begins.

> One feather, and the house, sinking, falling, would have
> turned and pitched downwards to the depths of darkness.
>
> (214)

The house is put in order and people return to it.

They return to the house on the island because 'certain rites' in honour of the dead have to be gone through. James and Cam resent being coerced by their father into performing these rites with him. Having thwarted his wife's wish to let her son go to the lighthouse ten years earlier Mr Ramsay will now take him there himself; moreover he will bear gifts to the

VIRGINIA WOOLF AND THE POETRY OF FICTION

lighthouse keeper – his wife had always organized these. In narrative terms the sail satisfies the desire expressed in the opening lines of the novel. Although Part III of the novel covers events that take place ten years after the events of Part I there is nevertheless a sense in which its essential function is to create another perspective of what had been enacted in Part I, or yet another perspective of the woman at the window. The links with the past are such that they, in a sense, enable the past to be reborn. The reality of Mrs Ramsay, the thing she would hand on to others, has to be brought into being. This is brought about through the ritual journey to the lighthouse, literally undertaken by Mr Ramsay and vicariously experienced by Lily Briscoe who captures it and fixes it in her painting. The restoration of the house was described, as we have seen, as 'some rusty birth'(216). And in the interval between the closing of the door on the restored house and the arrival of the first of the visitors, there are hints in the atmosphere that suggest a new urge towards a harmonizing presence:

> And now ... there rose that half-heard melody, that intermittent music which the ear half catches but lets fall... the jar of a dor beetle, the squeak of a wheel, loud, low, but mysteriously related....
>
> (218)

The mysterious relation between the present and the past has to be understood.

On her first morning at the house Lily finds the absence of Mrs Ramsay everywhere in evidence. Tempers are frayed, no one knows what to take to the lighthouse, and there is no one to soothe Mr Ramsay. Lily fails him when he comes to her asking for sympathy. The whole situation is viewed through Lily's consciousness in images of emptiness and incoherence that emphasize the absence of Mrs Ramsay. It is

> as if the link that usually bound things together had been cut, and they floated up here, down there, off, anyhow. How aimless it was, how chaotic, how unreal it was, she thought, looking at her empty coffee cup.
>
> (227)

112

TO THE LIGHTHOUSE: AN ELEGY

She then tries to make some kind of sense of what is going on around her, and she does this by trying to give it all a shape.

> But what does one send to the Lighthouse? Perished. Alone. The grey-green light on the wall opposite. The empty places. Such were some of the parts, but how bring them together? she asked. As if any interruption would break the frail shape she was building on the table she turned her back to the window lest Mr. Ramsay should see her.
>
> (228)

She is, in other words, trying to connect the past to the present, by bringing different aspects of both into harmony with each other. This reminds her of the picture she had never finished; she sets to work on it again, positioning her easel on the lawn where it had stood ten years earlier. And she remembers the specific painterly problem she had then been trying to solve as she observed the woman in the window reading a fairy story to her little son.

> There was the wall; the hedge; the tree. The question was of some relation between those masses....
>
> (229)

and

> There was ... something she remembered in the relations of those lines cutting across, slicing down, and in the mass of the hedge with its green cave of blues and browns....
>
> (243)

In working on this painting Lily enlarges her original vision, and in doing so she relives imaginatively moments from the past that had contributed to its meaning. In this way Mrs Ramsay is brought to life again in her consciousness. As she paints she loses consciousness of outer things: memories of the past, usually in the form of composed scenes featuring the presence of Mrs Ramsay, come flooding into her mind. One such grouping is of herself and Charles Tansley on the beach with Mrs Ramsay watching them as they are throwing stones – a scene

VIRGINIA WOOLF AND THE POETRY OF FICTION

which survived, after all these years, complete, so that she dipped into it to re-fashion her memory of him, and it stayed in the mind almost like a work of art.

(248–9)

It was Mrs Ramsay who had preserved it:

Mrs. Ramsay making of the moment something permanent (as in another sphere Lily herself tried to make of the moment something permanent) – this was of the nature of a revelation.

(249)

The great revelation for Lily is that Mrs Ramsay had been able to strike into stability something that was 'passing and flowing', and that her gift of being able to harmonize the elements of 'life' into a whole was similar to her own gift of being able to make the parts cohere into a whole in her paintings. In abstract terms the revelation that had come to her from Mrs Ramsay is 'In the midst of chaos there was shape...' (249).

As Lily takes stock of her painting she expresses her thoughts in the same images she had used ten years earlier, but the advance in her painting has been considerable. Then

She could have wept. It was bad, it was bad, it was infinitely bad!... She saw the colour burning on a framework of steel; the light of a butterfly's wing lying upon the arches of a cathedral. Of all that only a few random marks scrawled upon the canvas remained.

(78)

Now she paints as one truly inspired:

The whole mass of the picture was poised upon that weight. Beautiful and bright it should be on the surface, feathery and evanescent, one colour melting into another like the colours on a butterfly's wing; but beneath the fabric must be clamped together with bolts of iron.

(264)

As the past is relived imaginatively the picture progresses; as Lily makes her journey back into the past she moves onwards in her painting. This is expressed in the image of a journey that takes her, on foot, out to sea:

TO THE LIGHTHOUSE: AN ELEGY

It was an odd road to be walking, this of painting. Out and
out one went, further and further, until at last one seemed
to be on a narrow plank, perfectly alone, over the sea.

(265)

So the past, Mrs Ramsay, the journey, the sea, the painting,
are all imaginatively fused as past and present come together.

One of the most significant stages accomplished by Lily in
her painting as she goes on 'tunnelling her way into her
picture, into the past'(267) is that in which she loses her
dependence on Mrs Ramsay. The dead woman relinquishes
her hold on her. Because she no longer has the power to
influence her, Lily reflects that 'She recedes further and further
from us'(269). Yet she would summon her back if she could.
Once she has attained that measure of freedom from the past
she is able to enlarge the scope of her painting. Its foundation
is still the image of the woman reading to her child, but what
is needed to complete it is Mr Ramsay. So Lily turns her
attention away from Mrs Ramsay whom she can still see 'at the
end of the corridor of years'(269) to the figure in the boat
whose journey is so closely linked to her own.

Mr Ramsay starts his journey in becalmed waters, as Lily
metaphorically does in her painting, and as Mrs Ramsay had
done at the beginning of the dinner party. But then the wind
suddenly catches the sails and off they shoot. That the journey
has to do with Mrs Ramsay is implied by the children's resentment of their father and 'those rites he went through for his
own pleasure in memory of dead people...'(255). The first
stage of his journey comes when he relinquishes his dream in
favour of reality, or when, in other words, he stops thinking of
his dead wife and of 'how he walked up and down between the
urns on the terrace; how the arms were stretched out to
him'(258), and with a gentler manner begins to be considerate
in his attitude to Cam.

When the boat is half-way across the bay the wind drops and
the sun shines hotly on them as the boat rocks in the becalmed
waters. With this lull tensions are released and 'everybody
seemed to come very close together and to feel each other's
presence'(282). This evokes the moment at the dinner party
when, with the lighting of the candles, 'faces on both sides of

115

the table were brought nearer'(152). It was the moment at which Mrs Ramsay had her transcendent experience of coherence at the heart of life. With this moment in the present James realizes that it is not his father he hates but only something in him. And Cam's resentment turns into admiration. As all three look back, literally and symbolically, from the boat to the island, the past ceases to disturb them. They make a new coherence of their lives by coming close to each other. James at last sails to the lighthouse, and Mr Ramsay, renewed and vigorous, steps ashore on to the rock. With their arrival Lily completes her picture.

Within the three-part structure of *To the Lighthouse* the core of the work lies in its opening section; at its centre is the woman in the window who has striven for and achieved a certain coherence at the heart of her life. Part I of the novel is rich and alive ultimately because there Mrs Ramsay is alive and richly generous in her gift of herself to others. Part II creates a vision of a world in which she is both literally and metaphorically absent, a world in which there is no coherence, one in which there is, instead, death and suffering, war and anguish. With telling simplicity the inarticulate Mrs McNab doing her best to clean the abandoned house comments that 'Things were better then than now'(212). The ritual that Mr Ramsay, the children, and Lily Briscoe go through in the final part of the novel is one of a journey to the past through memory whereby they reach a position of peace and stability in the present. They have to confront the past, the woman in the window, in order to lay the ghosts of the past. The closure of the novel is one of arrival and completion.

Chapter Six

THE WAVES: A PLAYPOEM

As early as 1923, as we have seen, Virginia Woolf's sense of the mystery of the universe and the complexity of human existence is bound up with her feelings for the sea. Her growing awareness of the 'poetry of existence' leads her increasingly to experiment with the poetic as a fictional mode. Her affinity with the sea stems from her childhood association with the sea at St Ives. The world of Talland House with the sea at the end of the garden and the lighthouse in the distance, the ramshackle house itself and the garden where the children played cricket and their parents walked in the summer evenings, remained always a golden world for her. A return to it through memory seemed always to bring her psychological and emotional reassurance, a kind of stability. It is as if, in looking back to that past, she touched something that was real and permanent at the base of her life. She could go back and back to 'significant moments' at St Ives for inspiration and revelation. *To the Lighthouse* embodies that past.

As a child Virginia Woolf did not, of course, understand the meaning of that experience, but only knew that something very special had happened to her. Half a century later she attempted to analyse those 'moments of being' connected with the sea and St Ives in 'A Sketch of the Past'. *To the Lighthouse* is structured round some of those 'moments of being'. *The Waves*, a more analytic and theoretic novel, attempts to convey more of the meaning behind the experience of transcendence in those 'moments'. *To the Lighthouse* is still a 'psychological' novel because, even though Mrs Ramsay reaches beyond the literal to what lies behind it, and Lily Briscoe has her vision, the experimental core of the work inheres in the processes of

117

VIRGINIA WOOLF AND THE POETRY OF FICTION

perception which the author conveys in her exploration of the human consciousness. *The Waves*, on the other hand, is a mystical work in which the emphasis is less on the actual processes of perception than on the understanding of the individual in terms of the universal and mysterious nature of human existence. This shift in focus enables Virginia Woolf to create what is her most obviously 'poetic' novel.

John Middleton Murry had said that there was no way of going on after *Jacob's Room*. Remembering this when struggling with *Mrs. Dalloway*, Virginia Woolf had certain misgivings about what she was doing. Nevertheless, she wrote in her diary:

> Yet if this book proves anything, it proves that I can only write along those lines, and shall never desert them, but explore further and further and shall, heaven be praised, never bore myself an instant.

> *(AWD: 63)*

All through her fictional career she would 'explore further and further'. The further stage after *Jacob's Room* was a more fully integrated work that was, as we have seen, a psychological novel. *Mrs. Dalloway* is Virginia Woolf's essentially 'psychological' novel because in that novel the perspective is more centrally on the individual human being. Any wider conclusions about the nature of life derive almost entirely from what has been revealed through the exploration of the individual consciousness on the one hand, and on the other hand from the way in which one consciousness impinges on another within human relationships.

In *To the Lighthouse* the perspective shifts so that the personal forces of life are set against the impersonal: the human, so closely viewed and experienced in the few hours of Part I of the novel, is placed against the backcloth of the historical and metaphysical in Part II, revealing the general implications of the individual and particular. This enlarged perspective is achieved through an increasingly poetic form of writing. *To the Lighthouse* is, therefore, a more symbolic work than *Mrs. Dalloway*. Virginia Woolf experiments further in *The Waves* by continuing along the new line of development begun in *To the Lighthouse*; she exploits the potential of the lyrical evocation of the passage of time in the central section of the earlier novel.

In *The Waves* she 'explores further and further' in two different directions, though both are connected. The one has to do with her new perspective of life, or the vision behind the novel: she moves from the particular to the general, from the concrete to the abstract; from the lives of people to life itself. The other has to do with language, with the medium through which she expresses her vision: she creates an elaborately formal style that is densely symbolic and richly poetic. *The Waves* is a mystical work that she called 'a playpoem'.

There is something absolute about this work by virtue of the mystical vision that informs it. It embodies the furthest reach of Virginia Woolf's transcendent awareness; it touches an experimental area beyond which it is impossible to go. In *The Waves* she has achieved the ultimate artistic embodiment of her ideal through a sustained fusion of thought and metaphor. She has embodied the most severely abstract conceptions in the most vivid and vibrant of images. She has so saturated the novel with poetry that it almost ceases to be a novel. An absolute unity is achieved between the vision and substance of the book and the medium through which it is expressed.

What gives this kind of coherence is something that when it is put into words sounds very simple. It is the awareness Virginia Woolf had all through her life that there was a point at which things would cohere and that it was this that gave life meaning. Mrs Ramsay had that awareness. Bernard in *The Waves* has it too, but he tries to understand it and to articulate it. The author explains her understanding of that awareness in her autobiographical work 'A Sketch of the Past'. The 'Sketch' holds the key to this most complex and difficult of her novels. Much critical attention has been given to its remarkable stylistic features, and also to its obvious and elaborate structural framework. It is, however, more difficult to elicit the central significance of the novel, its poetic conception and the sustained poetical realization of its vision.

The first glimpses of that vision came to Virginia Woolf when she was writing *To the Lighthouse*. One indication of this is her admission that she had become possessed by a new searching spirit. She wanted to find a reality beyond the ordinariness of daily life, or something beyond, even, its bright moments of excitement and fulfilment.

VIRGINIA WOOLF AND THE POETRY OF FICTION

> I enjoy almost everything. Yet I have some restless searcher
> in me. Why is there not a discovery in life? Something one
> can lay hands on and say "This is it"? My depression is a
> harassed feeling. I'm looking: but that's not it – that's not it.
> What is it? And shall I die before I find it?
>
> (*A WD*: 86)

Virginia Woolf puts the 'restless searcher' of her self into
the central section of *To the Lighthouse* as the mystic wanderer
on the shore who asks the same questions she had asked and
recorded in her diary shortly before writing that section of the
novel:

> Meanwhile the mystic, the visionary, walked the beach,
> stirred a puddle, looked at a stone, and asked themselves
> "What am I?" "What is this?" and suddenly an answer was
> vouchsafed them (what it was they could not say): so that
> they were warm in the frost and had comfort in the desert.
>
> (*TL*: 203–4)

When she had finished *To the Lighthouse* Virginia Woolf
wrote again of her mystical feelings, revealing more about
their nature and meaning. This, she says, was for her a whole
new area of experience:

> I wished to add some remarks to this, on the mystical side of
> this solicitude; how it is not oneself but something in the
> universe that one's left with. It is this that is frightening and
> exciting in the midst of my profound gloom, depression,
> boredom, whatever it is. One sees a fin passing far out. What
> image can I reach to convey what I mean? Really there is
> none, I think. The interesting thing is that in all my feeling
> and thinking I have never come up against this before. Life
> is, soberly and accurately, the oddest affair; has in it the
> essence of reality.
>
> (*A WD*: 101)

What Virginia Woolf is after, then, is 'the essence of reality',
and the image that represents that for her is the 'fin' passing
far out at sea. She wonders if this experience will be the
starting point for a novel. 'I hazard the guess that it may be
the impulse behind another book' (30 September 1926; *A WD*:

120

THE WAVES: A PLAYPOEM

102); three weeks later she writes that she is haunted by 'some semi-mystical very profound life of a woman'. Six months after that she speaks of resting her head 'before starting the very serious, mystical poetical work which I want to come next' (*AWD*: 105). Two years later *The Waves,* which she had first thought of as *The Moths,* still hovers at the back of her mind; it is still not ready to be written. Her preparation for beginning it seems to be a continued examination of her own mystical feelings. She writes in September 1928, for instance:

> Often down there [at Rodmell] I have entered into a
> sanctuary; a nunnery; had a religious retreat; of great agony
> once; and always some terror; so afraid one is of loneliness;
> of seeing to the bottom of the vessel. That is one of the
> experiences I have had here in some Augusts; and got then
> to a consciousness of what I call "reality": a thing I see
> before me: something abstract; but residing in the downs or
> sky; beside which nothing matters; in which I shall rest and
> continue to exist. Reality I call it.
>
> (*AWD*: 132)

A high price has to be paid, then, in order to achieve this kind of awareness. It takes effort. Virginia Woolf has had to endure the anguish of 'seeing to the bottom' of her self in order to discover and confront her own reality. That seems to be a prerequisite for the glimpse that is awarded to her of the greater reality which is outside the self but in which she is also caught up. It is what happens to Bernard in the 'Eclipse' section of his 'summing up'.

In November 1928 she tentatively describes the book that might be an expression of her new mystical feelings ('That was to be an abstract mystical eyeless book: a playpoem' – *AWD*: 137) with an interesting reference to the form it might take should she write it: she might harness her poetic mode of expression to the dramatic, hence the name 'playpoem'. She goes on to conclude with a certain circularity of thought that if she wrote that book she would be forced to 'come to terms with these mystical feelings'. The subject of *The Waves* is, therefore, firmly established; its form is just beginning to emerge. Essentially, this will be a more poetically sustained work than anything she has yet attempted:

121

VIRGINIA WOOLF AND THE POETRY OF FICTION

The idea has come to me that what I want now to do is to saturate every atom. I mean to eliminate all waste, deadness, superfluity: to give the moment whole; whatever it includes. Say that the moment is a combination of thought; sensation; the voice of the sea. Waste, deadness, come from the inclusion of things that don't belong to the moment; this appalling narrative business of the realist: getting on from lunch to dinner: it is false, unreal, merely conventional. Why admit anything to literature that is not poetry – by which I mean saturated? Is that not my grudge against novelists? that they select nothing? The poets succeeding by simplifying: practically everything is left out. I want to put practically everything in: yet to saturate.

(*AWD*: 139)

Virginia Woolf records in her diary several of her attempts to find the right form for her vision. The following is one of the more interesting instances:

I am not trying to tell a story. Yet perhaps it might be done in that way. A mind thinking. They might be islands of light – islands in the stream that I am trying to convey; life itself going on.

(*AWD*: 142–3)

When the novel is finished she notes that in writing it she had been searching for the 'vision' she had had at Rodmell in the summer months after she had completed *To the Lighthouse*. So we have come full circle. The elusive nature of reality, or 'the essence of reality' that one might come across unbidden in the sky, on the downs, or in the shifting light on the sea, and which Virginia Woolf called 'a fin passing far out' has in some measure, after four years of searching, been reached. Or, as she acknowledged nearly a year later, in February 1931: 'I have netted that fin in the waste of water which appeared to me over the marshes out of my window at Rodmell when I was coming to an end of *To the Lighthouse*' (*AWD*: 169).

To summarize, then. Authorial intention, as it is revealed in her diary, is to convey in a work of fiction 'the essence of reality', or symbolically, to net 'the fin in a waste of water'. The novel is to be a 'playpoem'. The 'poetry' is assigned to the

122

interspersed Interludes, and the 'play' or dramatic element is put into the elaborately structured series of soliloquies which embody the lives of the six characters. There are two aspects to her method of characterization. One is that her people are to be more like caricatures, created in a few bold strokes (*A WD*: 157). The other is that their lives are to be built up through a mode of narration that is as far removed from realist narrative methods as possible. They are to be conveyed through a series of significant moments, or 'moments of being'. She wants to 'give the moment whole', to cut out from this novel everything that is not poetry. Nearly everything that Virginia Woolf 'says' in this novel is expressed through imagery. And even in her discussion of its structure she relies on images to express her ideas: she wants to create 'islands of light in the stream of life'. The conception of the book's structure is, therefore, essentially an abstract one, one of design or pattern. The outer framework embodies the universal or life in general (the stream), and its controlling imagery is that of the waves. The individual and specific is embodied in the 'moments' of being or wholeness that are conveyed in the soliloquies (islands of light). In this way Virginia Woolf seeks to convey her mystical sense of the otherness of life, of her 'astonishing sense of something there, which is "it" ', and of her own relatedness to it.

The claim that 'A Sketch' holds the key to *The Waves* might on the face of it seem an exaggeration. All fiction is in a sense autobiographical. But the middle period of Virginia Woolf's fiction more than any other draws on her own psychological investigation of her own past. It is generally recognized that in *To the Lighthouse* she has recreated the golden world of her childhood. But it is less obvious that *The Waves* is also based on it. In *The Waves* she returns to that same world for different reasons and from a different vantage point. As her vision became wider, more mystical, and in consequence more philosophical, she looked back to the past through the lens of that mysticism to see it differently and also to understand and possibly find explanations. It is for this reason that 'A Sketch' is so important. The more attentively one reads it the better one will understand *The Waves*. 'A Sketch' is a kind of psychological–philosophical autobiography built in the main out of an

VIRGINIA WOOLF AND THE POETRY OF FICTION

analysis of significant 'moments' from her past through which she constructs a 'life' of her self. This is in fact what Bernard does in *The Waves*. 'A Sketch' is, therefore, very like the novel, only it is not, as the novel is, written in the poetic mode.

Two of the 'moments' recounted in 'A Sketch' have, I believe, an essential connection with *The Waves*. The first has to do with the nursery at St Ives which was fictionally recreated in *To the Lighhouse*. Virginia Woolf said that it was the most important of all her memories.

> If life has a base that it stands upon, if it is a bowl that one fills and fills and fills – then my bowl without a doubt stands upon this memory. It is of lying half asleep, half awake, in bed in the nursery at St. Ives. It is of hearing the waves breaking, one, two, one, two, and sending a splash of water over the beach; and then breaking, one, two, one, two, behind a yellow blind. It is of hearing the blind draw its little acorn across the floor as the wind blew the blind out. It is of lying and hearing this splash and seeing this light, and feeling, it is almost impossible that I should be here; of feeling the purest ecstasy I can conceive.

> (*MB*: 64–5)

This experience lies behind *The Waves*. The first Interlude of *The Waves*, for instance, describes the sun rising over the sea and concludes with reference to the blind stirring at the nursery bedroom window. The first soliloquy opens with children waking up in the nursery. But the experience is also the great archetypal base on which the novel as a whole stands; Bernard begins his summing up by going back to their first conscious moments in the nursery. 'In the beginning, there was the nursery, with windows opening on to a garden, and beyond that the sea' (169). Through the biblical allusiveness of the opening phrase Bernard at once mythologizes and universalizes their individual experience. As he goes on to recount his earliest recollections he says: 'All these things happen in one second and last for ever' (170). This is an essential truth that Virginia Woolf is exploring in 'A Sketch', and is the rationale behind the structure of both it and the novel.

The other 'moment' from 'A Sketch' also connected with St Ives is of a different nature. Virginia Woolf writes:

124

THE WAVES: A PLAYPOEM

> I was looking at the flower by the front door; "That is the whole" I said. I was looking at a plant with a spread of leaves; and it seemed suddenly plain that the flower itself was a part of the earth; that a ring enclosed what was the flower; and that was the real flower; part earth; part flower. It was a thought I put away as being likely to be very useful to me later.
>
> (*MB*: 71)

This is a moment of transcendence, of a mystical sense of something existing beyond the literal and tangible object one is looking at. Embedded in this vision is a realization of the meaning and importance of wholeness; that something is made whole often through the inclusion of something else which is not essentially of itself. When this understanding came to Virginia Woolf as a child it at once resolved itself into the symbol of a ring.

The experience recorded with such simplicity of language here is in reality very complex, and is actually the central experience, the recurring experience which is endlessly recollected and examined, in *The Waves.*

In the first moment, in which she as an individual is caught up in the rhythm of the waves breaking on the shore outside the nursery window, Virginia Woolf found the symbol of the waves which she exploits to its fullest extent in the novel of that name. It is the symbol of life itself, the great universal which contains and sustains the individual. In the second moment, in which she recognizes the importance of wholeness and coherence, she finds the symbol of the ring or circle, which is the symbol of wholeness, of containment, of eternity, and it too recurs throughout the novel. Bernard, the central character of the novel, the one who is eventually able to sum up the others and make a whole out of their lives ('this globe, full of figures': 169) wakes up in the nursery: ' "I see a ring," said Bernard, "hanging above me. It quivers and hangs in a loop of light" ' (6). This recalls a famous poetic image of eternity:

> I saw Eternity the other night
> Like a great Ring of pure and endless light,
>   All calm as it was bright...
>
> (Henry Vaughan, 'The World')

125

Bernard, like all the characters in the novel, tries to make things come together in a sequence, or a globe, or a circle, or a ring, all variations of the same image. Louis, for instance, wants to preserve the moment of the cricket match. He does so by embodying it in a poem. He and the other children are literally sitting in a circle on the grass. But for him the occasion is special and the little group has an aura of the eternal about it:

> Now grass and trees ... and our ring here, sitting, with our arms binding our knees, hint at some other order, and better, which makes a reason everlastingly. This I see for a second, and shall try to-night to fix in words, to forge in a ring of steel....
>
> (28)

Louis, who all his life feels solitary and excluded, will preserve this moment of integration by putting a ring round it. This 'moment' enables him to detect wholeness, or at least recognize the possibility of coherence, in unlikely places in later life. As a successful city businessman he enters an eating-house 'conscious of flux, of disorder; of annihilation and despair', and in this he is very like Rhoda whose attitude to life is similarly dark. But unlike her he has the ability to make things cohere for himself; he can connect with some real thing in the external world, which saves him from disintegration, and he can draw meaning from experiences in the past. This is what is happening as he responds to the rhythm of the eating-house:

> Where then is the break in this continuity? What the fissure through which one sees disaster? The circle is unbroken; the harmony complete. Here is the central rhythm; here the common mainspring. I watch it expand, contract; and then expand again. Yet I am not included.
>
> (68)

At this point, recognizing the 'circle', he summons up moments of being from his childhood, and the reality he touched in them, the sense of something eternal he had found in that experience, is brought forward from the past into the present to be experienced again in the eating-house.

THE WAVES: A PLAYPOEM

I woke in a garden with a blow on the nape of my neck, a
hot kiss, Jinny's.... I see the gleaming tea-urn; the glass cases
full of pale-yellow sandwiches; the men in round coats
perched on stools at the counter; and also behind them,
eternity.

(69)

Behind the present lies the past. In this way, as in *A Sketch*,
'moments of being' continue into the present, grow, and
accumulate about them new layers of meaning. For all the
characters in the novel they last a lifetime and enrich their
lives.

Jinny is able to make a whole out of what is around her
through her own inner energy, though the kind of coherence
she finds in life is of a more limited nature:

When I came in just now everything stood still in a
pattern.... I can imagine nothing beyond the circle cast by
my body. My body goes before me, like a lantern down a
dark lane, bringing one thing after another out of darkness
into a ring of light.

(92)

For Rhoda, who is unable to establish a coherence in life, for
whom, in other words, the moments are not strong enough to
form a continuum, there is only despair. When she finally
admits that 'The circle is destroyed. We are thrown asunder' (102)
she takes her own life.

It is, however, the shadowy charismatic figure of Percival
who by the potency of his being is able to unite all the
characters into a whole through his silent presence. They all
become complete persons through what he is, much as the
flower in the garden at St Ives became whole by virtue of
being part of the earth. The farewell dinner for Percival is a
festival (Neville uses the word), a kind of ritual celebration of
his place in their lives. The group is again united as it had
been on the cricket field at school. They are now in their mid-
twenties. And the image that expresses the whole that they
form is a flower, 'a seven-sided flower, many-petalled, red,
puce, purple-shaded, stiff with silver-tinted leaves – a whole
flower to which every eye brings its own contribution' (91).

VIRGINIA WOOLF AND THE POETRY OF FICTION

All achieve a sense of wholeness at this celebratory meal. All seem to touch a reality or a significance beyond what they are all literally engaged in doing. They all attribute this to the 'moment of being' corporately created for them by the real presence of Percival whom Bernard refers to as a God. At one point Rhoda thinks of him as a great stone in a pond round which minnows swarm, and that like the minnows they 'undulate and eddy contentedly'(98). 'The world that had been shrivelled, rounds itself' because of his presence. And Louis who recalls how Percival had at school sat among them in the grass thinks of 'a steel-blue circle beneath', the image he had then used in trying to fix that moment in a poem.

Through both Louis' and Rhoda's heightened imagination the occasion takes on a primitive aspect. This serves to articulate the primitive feelings roused in all of them by Percival's presence. In both instances the symbolism of the ring is retained:

> "Like the dance of savages," said Louis, "round the camp-fire. They are savage; they are ruthless. They dance in a circle, flapping bladders. The flames leap over their painted faces, over the leopard skins and the bleeding limbs which they have torn from the living body."
>
> "The flames of the festival rise high," said Rhoda. "The great procession passes, flinging green boughs and flowering branches. Their horns spill blue smoke; their skins are dappled red and yellow in the torchlight. They throw violets. They deck the beloved with garlands and with laurel leaves, there on the ring of turf where the steep-backed hills come down. The procession passes...."

> (100–1)

Rhoda's vision of Percival is, however, fraught with implicit foreboding: she will herself soon throw violets as a tribute to him, when she has learnt of his sudden death. As if unconsciously confirming this Louis says 'Death is woven in with the violets'(101).

Special though this 'moment of being', this awareness of wholeness, is, it must none the less like all the others come to an end. Some try to prolong it. Louis, feeling that 'the circle in our blood... closes in a ring', pleads silently 'Do not move, do

128

THE WAVES: A PLAYPOEM

not let the swing door cut to pieces the thing that we have made, that globes itself here.... Hold it for ever'(104). And Jinny similarly asks that 'this globe whose walls are made of Percival might be held a little longer'(104). Bernard, the phrase-maker, who tries to understand experience by putting it into words, acknowledges matter-of-factly that the moment is over, but he adds cryptically that 'what is to come is in it'(104). The reader learns in the 'summing up' that all that occurs in the present, or will occur in the future, had been there implicitly in the past.

Virginia Woolf makes the point, in her autobiographical sketch, that 'moments of being' are very few in life, most of life being made up of long stretches of 'non-being': 'These separate moments of being were however embedded in many more moments of non-being'(*MB*: 70). Novels of realism are mostly built out of vast tracts of non-being. This is what she refers to in her diary as the 'appalling narrative business of the realist', and what she cuts out of this novel, choosing instead to make a 'narrative' out of selected 'moments of being'. She wants to give 'the moment whole'. And the whole moment is 'a combination of thought; sensation; the voice of the sea'. This is also the simple essence of this complex novel, which is after all a presentation of thought and sensation through images, out of which some synthesis, such as Bernard attempts in his summing up, might be made. This is what a 'de-construction' of the text would resolve itself into.

The whole thrust of this novel is towards a few simple ideas or propositions at the centre of which is the urge towards wholeness that is so much in evidence at Percival's farewell dinner. These might be summarized as follows. Each human being's existence is separate and indivisible. Yet human beings can only achieve wholeness of being through their capacity to emerge from their separateness into a sense of relatedness to other human beings and to the world around them. To a greater or lesser extent, according to their inner resources, they are able to penetrate further both into the world around them, or even further beyond its bounds to a sense of the universe, the cosmos, or to life itself. Similarly, to a greater or lesser extent, they are able to realize the mystery of their own individual existences by finding a unifying principle within

VIRGINIA WOOLF AND THE POETRY OF FICTION

their own lives, and by reaching some understanding of how their own uniqueness is not something that exists in total isolation from others or from the universe, but which is instead one that is established and defined by virtue of their achieved harmony with both the human environment and the natural and cosmic environment. And at the centre of all this can be detected the binary opposition of order and chaos, the eternal and the temporal. All the lives are played out against and within that reality. It is what underlies the account of the dawn in the opening Interlude in which sea, land, and sky become differentiated as light and dark are divided. Here, of course, there are hints too of the account of the creation in Genesis whereby God divided the sea and the land and brought order out of chaos:

> The sea was indistinguishable from the sky, except that the sea was slightly creased as if a cloth had wrinkles in it. Gradually as the sky whitened a dark line lay on the horizon dividing the sea from the sky and the grey cloth became barred with thick strokes moving, one after another, beneath the surface, following each other, pursuing each other, perpetually.

(5)

The essential struggle of all humanity is to escape from chaos through order, the mark of which is a sense of wholeness which might be symbolized, for instance, by the ring or circle. This abstract concept is at the heart of *The Waves* though it is deeply embedded in layer upon layer of imagery. The six characters grow and develop between the polarities of order and chaos; the pattern of their lives emerges out of the process through which they negotiate those opposing forces, succumbing to chaos or surviving it as they acquire and develop their individual means of creating order.

These individual lives are presented in soliloquy. Each character articulates his or her thought and conveys his or her feelings in a poetic monologue. These monologues are organized into the nine 'ages of man' from childhood to old age, and all move forward in time concurrently. Bernard, one of the six, speaks for them all, so that their separate lives are summed up, or unified, through his voice. He is the phrase-maker.

130

THE WAVES: A PLAYPOEM

The nine sections of the novel embodying the different phases of human development are interspersed with poetic Interludes that trace the movement of the sun through the sky in the course of one day. That movement reflects the rise and fall of human life from infancy to old age. The two strands of the novel are fused together poetically through, in particular, the pervading movement and symbolism of the waves which form both. Increasingly, as the characters grow older, what is stated in the Interludes and what is explored in the soliloquies merge. This is because the Interludes embody primarily the general and universal in life through their descriptions of the universe, the cosmos, human existence in its entirety. As man grows older and develops and becomes individualized, he at the same time becomes increasingly aware of his place in the wider context of the universe, and, in metaphysical terms, of the universal. The two merge completely at the end in Bernard's summing up.

The characters who speak their soliloquies in this novel and whose individual lives are revealed through them are not rounded or fully achieved characters. Instead, Virginia Woolf created what she called 'caricatures' through a few bold strokes. They are types who fit into the general schematic framework of this highly patterned work. They are all, after the manner of Virginia Woolf herself, 'restless searchers' who look for, and sometimes detect, the 'fin in a waste of water'. They are equally divided into three male and three female characters. Of the three female characters the most complex and important is Rhoda, a visionary, who in her thoughts and general cast of mind, much resembles the author. Jinny, the vital feminine figure lives essentially through her body in a succession of affairs with different men. She is a city dweller. In contrast Susan finds fulfilment in marriage and motherhood as a farmer's wife. She is a country dweller. These three characters are each connected with one of the elements, water, fire, and earth respectively.

Jinny is the figure of fire and is usually associated with the colour red. 'I leap like one of those flames that run between the cracks of the earth; I move, I dance' (30), she thinks. As a child she dreams that when she is grown up she will wear a thin dress 'shot with red threads that would gleam in the

VIRGINIA WOOLF AND THE POETRY OF FICTION

firelight'(24), and sit on a gilt chair in the middle of a room. This image of how she would centre her own life, unify it through her own sexual vitality, is also how the other characters see her when they think of her. As they analyse her they define their own characters through what she is and what she is not.

Susan is the figure of earth. As a child she makes images of what she hates and buries them in the ground. She would bury the whole school if she could. Her freedom unfurls when she is able to escape to the country. She finds fulfilment close to the soil and contentment among her children and her animals. Symbolically she identifies herself with the land and the cycles of nature. 'At this hour, this still early hour, I think I am the field, I am the barn, I am the trees.... I am the seasons, I think sometimes, January, May, November; the mud, the mist, the dawn'(70–1).

Rhoda is the figure of water. As a child she rocks her white petals in her brown basin: 'So that my ships may ride the waves. Some will founder. Some will dash themselves against the cliffs. One sails alone. That is my ship'(13). She is a solitary figure, feeling always threatened by others, yet it is paradoxically her communication with others that saves her for so long from succumbing to the fragmentariness of life, the chaos. Eventually she does succumb and commits suicide. Her fear is always: 'I ride rough waters and shall sink with no one to save me'(114). To Bernard she is 'the nymph of the fountain always wet'(84).

The three male characters are not so systematically differentiated, though they are quite different kinds of people. Louis, the son of a Brisbane banker, is an outsider figure. He feels socially inferior to the others because of his Australian accent which represents their cultural differences. He compensates for his social inadequacies and his deep-seated sense of isolation by achieving success in the world of commerce. He does not, however, become completely worldly since he keeps his 'attic room' where he writes poetry. He and Rhoda become lovers. Neville, the classicist, becomes a university don. He is a secretive private person who values solitude, though he likes to have one person with whom he can share it. He had loved Percival. That love is kept alive as he takes up other lovers.

THE WAVES: A PLAYPOEM

Bernard is the most important of the six characters. He becomes a novelist. As the story-teller and phrase-maker he reaches to the meaning of experience through his ability to put it into words. He does this most completely in his summing up at the end of the novel.

The premise on which Bernard's summing up stands is the one that Virginia Woolf affirms in 'A Sketch', and it incidentally validates this long investigation into the origins of her visionary awareness:

> The illusion is upon me that something adheres for a
> moment, has roundness, weight, depth, is completed. This,
> for the moment, seems to be my life.
>
> (168–9)

He addresses the reader as an imaginary companion at the restaurant table. The image he uses to express the completeness of his life, its wholeness, is the now familiar one associated with him of a globe or a globe-shaped object. The round thing that he sees as his life is full of figures. To explain this to his companion he must tell a story, the story of his life. He begins at the beginning and recounts in a condensed form, and from the perspective of his search for his own identity, the lives of the others. These are the people who had figured in his childhood and whom he had occasionally met again in the course of his life. He had put a circle round them; and they had remained always with him: 'It is as if one had woken in Stonehenge surrounded by a circle of great stones, these enemies, these presences'(171). The beginning is the nursery, and by using the opening words of St John's Gospel which reach back to the origins of life in eternity he endows the personal account of his own origins with archetypal significance: 'In the beginning, there was the nursery, with windows opening on to a garden, and beyond that the sea'(169). As he recalls his past he mythologizes it.

Summing up each stage of his life he notes the pain that seems to be involved as the self gradually evolves: 'We suffered terribly as we became separate bodies'(171). Most obviously the self grows through 'moments of being', but it also evolves through long periods of non-being, such as the time spent at school. He remembers the dullness and monotony of school life as a time when: 'Nothing, nothing, nothing broke with its fin that leaden waste of waters' (174).

When he thinks of adolescence he remembers a scene by a river in which his attention had been drawn away from his personal preoccupations to the beauty of the natural world around him. In his response to that beauty another dimension was added to his awareness – the possibility of permanence. This meaning inheres for him in the object (the willow that grows on the turf by the river) that gave rise to the experience. As he remembers the willow the meaning comes back to him; he is redirected by it 'to that which is beyond and outside our own predicament; to that which is symbolic...' (176). With this thought he brings the whole scene back to life imaginatively, with Neville, Rhoda and Jinny. It shapes itself into the reality of the present, and he now places round it symbolically a ring of light: 'There was no past, no future; merely the moment in its ring of light, and our bodies; and the inevitable climax, the ecstasy' (179). This is a moment of wholeness that transcends the bounds of time and will remain with him for ever.

Bernard continually oscillates between the polarized worlds of the visionary and the literal or mundane, the past and the present, the eternal and the temporal. Through this process he reaches an understanding of life and ultimately synthesizes the various levels of existence and experience into the complete globe or ring of existence:

> The crystal, the globe of life as one calls it, far from being hard and cold to the touch, has walls of thinnest air. If I press them all will burst. Whatever sentence I extract whole and entire from this cauldron is only a string of six little fish that let themselves be caught....

> (182)

Within the globe: 'Faces recur, faces and faces – they press their beauty to the walls of my bubble – Neville, Susan, Louis, Jinny, Rhoda and a thousand others' (182). He defines himself against these and other faces as he has done constantly throughout his life (and as they also have done with each other in the course of the novel). So he reflects 'Louis, the

THE WAVES: A PLAYPOEM

attic dweller; Rhoda, the nymph of the fountain always wet; both contradicted what was then so positive to me...'(183).

All the figures in the globe had found something that 'stood them in good stead'. This is why he goes back to them again and again, to see if, imaginatively, he can elicit from them yet more of their reality. 'Thus I visited each of my friends in turn, trying, with fumbling fingers, to prise open their locked caskets'(189).

As he goes through his past, and through their lives, Bernard attaches to them something of his adult understanding. Thus he brings the past into the present, interpreting it with the knowledge that comes with age and experience:

> But I now made the contribution of maturity to childhood's intuitions – satiety and doom; the sense of what is unescapable in our lot; death; the knowledge of limitations; how life is more obdurate than one had thought it.
>
> (190–1)

Life can be 'obdurate' and the experience of that obduracy marks the point at which disintegration is closest. But at that point his spirit is able to rally and fight in order to piece together the fragments of his shattered existence. He makes things cohere again through language: 'I retrieved them from formlessness with words'(191).

Each time he summons up his various friends, and different situations, the order and shape of his life alters slightly. In this way life is rather like a kaleidoscope; with each shake the pattern changes though the pieces making up the pattern are always the same. So he wonders if it is not after all an illusion to think that there is one final or absolute design or order to be discovered: 'Time has given the arrangement another shake. Out we creep from the arch of the currant leaves, out into a wider world'(193).

Neville's friendship is one that Bernard has always valued highly. Neville understands him; they can communicate intellectually together. It is Neville who helps him to see a little further. He recalls, for instance, an occasion on which he had visited Neville in his tidy room, and they had sat by the fire and talked intimately together. He remembers how they had talked and then sank into one of those silences which are now and again broken by a few words, as if a fin rose in the wastes of silence; and then the fin, the thought, sinks back into the depths, spreading round it a little ripple of satisfaction, content.

(193–4)

He often re-creates such moments imaginatively, thus reliving the experience. But sometimes they come to him unbidden, as when, for example, he is walking through the London streets.

Bernard's major preoccupation during his long association with his friends has to do with the difficulty he finds in establishing his own true identity. His identity includes them; they have become part of his being because he has known them all his life, but, realizing this, he is unable to distinguish the demarcation of his 'real' self: 'I am not one person; I am many people; I do not altogether know who I am – Jinny, Susan, Neville, Rhoda, or Louis; or how to distinguish my life from theirs'(196). With this disturbing thought he summons back a moment in which they had all met together. But not only does he recall the gathering at Hampton Court, he recalls also his own perceptions of it, what he had then thought and felt, so that he can bring it to bear on the present. Essentially what he recalls is that they had together formed a kind of corporate idealized human being:

We saw for a moment laid out among us the body of the complete human being whom we have failed to be, but at the same time, cannot forget. All that we might have been we saw; all that we had missed, and we grudged for a moment the other's claim, as children when the cake is cut, the one cake, the only cake, watch their slice diminishing.

(196)

The dark implications of this moment of unification are that it reveals to him what he is not, or what he might have been. On a different level, however, it contains his awareness of something larger than himself in which he was caught up, and which has the quality of eternity about it: 'We were extinguished for a moment....' This experience of transcendence, like all the others in this book, lasts only for a second. After it

THE WAVES: A PLAYPOEM

is past he and his friends return to the more limited confines of the self: 'We became six people at a table in Hampton Court.'(197)

After reliving this moment Bernard goes on to reflect on its meaning and implications for himself. In that moment they had been united and had transcended the limitations of time and personality. So moments from the past can be retrieved in the present and can continue into the future: 'But we... for one moment out of what measureless abundance of past time and time to come, burnt there triumphant'(197). At the end of his reflections the moment dissolves itself back into the continuum of his life and is represented by the constant ebb and flow of the waves. Whenever he or any of the figures in the globe glimpses something that is eternal and enduring the image of the waves enters the discourse. So, when the moment is over, 'Neville, Jinny, Susan and I, as a wave breaks, burst asunder, surrendered... to the lights twisted like white ribbon on rippled waters'(197).

On this occasion he speaks of their having returned from 'that immersion' and come to the surface, as if experience had in it something of the nature of a baptism. And he realizes that he has to tug himself away from that 'immersion' in the eternal waters in order to become himself again, separate and unique. His entire thought is conveyed in images of the waters:

> I could not recover myself from that endless throwing away, dissipation flooding forth... over the roughened water to become waves in the sea – I could not recover myself from that dissipation.
>
> (198)

This moment had also been summoned back on subsequent occasions. In a reflective mood in a hairdresser's chair, for instance, he had tried to tease out its meaning and had come to the conclusion that even though he had had moments of vision he was not himself a mystic. Rhoda was, and she had killed herself. So he imaginatively summons her out of the globe as part of his life, the part he is able to master by making up phrases.

VIRGINIA WOOLF AND THE POETRY OF FICTION

In persuading her I was also persuading my own soul. For this is not one life; nor do I always know if I am man or woman, Bernard or Neville, Louis, Susan, Jinny, or Rhoda – so strange is the contact of one with another.

(199)

As he continues to relive and analyse moments from the past in this way he eventually does come close to some realization of his own identity.

Reassuring visions do not, however, come automatically to Bernard as soon as he looks into his globe full of figures. As if to illustrate this he recounts the part of his story that begins 'For one day as I leant over a gate that led into a field, the rhythm stopped...'(201). This initiates a moment that Christian mystics would describe as 'the dark night of the soul'. All he experiences is emptiness and negation. 'I waited. I listened. Nothing came, nothing.... No fin breaks the waste of this immeasurable sea'(201). His 'self' is negated. He has no identity. It is like an eclipse of the sun. In one of the most poetically charged passages in the novel he contemplates his past, his friends, yet again:

The woods had vanished; the earth was a waste of shadow. No sound broke the silence of the wintry landscape. No cock crowed; no smoke rose; no train moved. A man without a self, I said. A heavy body leaning on a gate. A dead man. With dispassionate despair, with entire disillusionment, I surveyed the dust dance; my life, my friends' lives, and those fabulous presences, men with brooms, women writing, the willow tree by the river – clouds and phantoms made of dust too, of dust that changed, as clouds lose and gain and take gold or red and lose their summits and billow this way and that, mutable, vain. I, carrying a notebook, making phrases, had recorded mere changes; a shadow, I had been sedulous to take note of shadows. How can I proceed now, I said, without a self, weightless and visionless, through a world weightless, without illusion?

(202–3)

The persons and the memories are now familiar to the reader. But here they are encountered in an unfamiliar perspective.

138

THE WAVES: A PLAYPOEM

Life has given way to death; they are all performing, suggestively, 'the dust dance' as if they had already been returned to the element out of which they had been made. They are shadows; selves without selves. To Bernard, who is now confronting his own death, life has become a wintry landscape, its path leading to 'more wintriness and pallor and the equal uninteresting view of the same landscape' (203). But as after an eclipse of the sun the light returns, so the darkness of winter is replaced by the light and hope of spring. After his 'dark night' the light returns to Bernard and he is, as it were, reborn into the world of light: 'So the landscape returned to me; so I saw fields rolling in waves of colour beneath me.... I walked alone in a new world, never trodden...' (203).

At the centre of his great vision at the end of his life is found the archetypal vision of its origins in the nursery with the garden and the sea, as at the centre of Virginia Woolf's vision recorded in her diary, analysed in 'A Sketch', and embodied in this novel, there was the nursery and the garden and the sea at St Ives. Bernard reflects:

> But for a moment I had sat on the turf somewhere high above the flow of the sea and the sound of the woods, had seen the house, the garden, and the waves breaking. The old nurse who turns the pages of the picture-book had stopped and had said, 'Look. This is the truth.'
>
> (204)

The end of Bernard's life, of all the lives contained in the globe full of figures, is the place where he had started to tell his story: 'In the beginning, there was the nursery, with windows opening on to a garden, and beyond that the sea' (169).

When Bernard has finished his story, when he is done with phrases and with all his surrogate selves, he is able to find continuance in the greater reality that is represented in the Interludes of the novel and is embodied in the waves. At the end the two worlds of the individual and the general, the specific and the universal, the eternal and the temporal, or, in other words, the soliloquies and the Interludes, merge in the eternal renewal of human existence:

139

VIRGINIA WOOLF AND THE POETRY OF FICTION

There is a sense of the break of day. I will not call it dawn. What is dawn in the city to an elderly man standing in the street looking up rather dizzily at the sky? Dawn is some sort of whitening of the sky; some sort of renewal. Another day; another Friday; another twentieth of March, January, or September. Another general awakening. The stars draw back and are extinguished. The bars deepen themselves between the waves.... Yes, this is the eternal renewal, the incessant rise and fall and fall and rise again.

And in me too the wave rises. It swells; it arches its back....

(210–11)

The Waves is a mystical poetical work of verbal complexity on a ground base of simplicity and profundity. This is what makes the book so difficult and demanding. The surface texture often bewilders and enthrals while below it, all the time, the 'restless searcher' merely seeks for the fin in the waste of waters, the sequence, the ring or the globe, or an equivalent form that might shape life meaningfully. What I have tried to indicate above all in my approach to *The Waves* is, in other words, that informing the virtuosity of this linguistic performance with its sustained intensity, with never a moment's give as the momentum builds up, is the simplicity of one large thought that is charted as it develops in the diary, which is analysed and assessed in 'A Sketch', and which is embodied in poetry in the novel that Virginia Woolf referred to as a 'playpoem'.

140

Chapter Seven

THE 'PURE POETRY' OF *BETWEEN THE ACTS*

When *The Years* was still at the novel-essay stage (December 1932), and was, therefore, a novel of 'fact', Virginia Woolf noted that her next novel would be a poetical one: 'Oh and I shall write a poet's book next. This one [*The Years*, at this stage called *The Pargiters*], however, releases such a torrent of fact as I did not know I had in me' (*AWD*: 190). *The Years* is followed by a poetical novel which is in some senses the most purely poetic of all Virginia Woolf's works. The Mallarméan use of the word 'pure' with its emphasis on a technically achieved unity dissociated from all authorial presence or personal voice expresses some of my meaning, though I am not suggesting that *Between the Acts* approaches or aspires to the Mallarméan ideal:

> If the poem is to be pure, the poet's voice must be stilled and the initiative taken by the words themselves, which will be set in motion as they meet unequally in collision. And in an enchange of gleams they will flame out like some glittering swath of fire sweeping over precious stones, and thus replace the audible breathing in lyric poetry of old – replace the poet's own personal and passionate control of verse.
>
> (Mallarmé, 'Crisis in Poetry': 40–1)

The Waves is generally acknowledged to be Virginia Woolf's greatest poetic achievement. Yet apart from its 'inner structures' it is the very 'passionate control' disclaimed by Mallarmé that sustains the verbal and emotional intensity of the writing and makes it the most powerful and demanding of her novels.

Between the Acts is a very different kind of novel. Its narrative proceeds in a light detached tone that flows easily and with

141

VIRGINIA WOOLF AND THE POETRY OF FICTION

considerable humour. It is ironic in the comedy of manners vein. Its tone is in large measure the tone of *Night and Day* and the openings of both novels are remarkably similar:

> It was a Sunday evening in October, and in common with many young ladies of her class, Katharine Hilbery was pouring out tea....
> Considering that the little party had been seated round the tea-table for less than twenty minutes, the animation observable on their faces, and the amount of sound they were producing collectively, were very creditable to the hostess.
>
> (*ND*: 1)

> It was a summer's night and they were talking in the big room with the windows open to the garden, about the cesspool....
> Mrs. Haines, the wife of the gentleman farmer, a goosefaced woman with eyes protruding as if they saw something to gobble in the gutter, said affectedly: "What a subject to talk about on a night like this!"
>
> (7)

Unlike *Night and Day*, however, *Between the Acts* is a short condensed novel. There is something quintessential about it, but without the relentless intensity of *The Waves*. It seems at times as if the initiative is 'taken by the words themselves', and that they 'meet in collision' – words, as I shall go on to show, like silence, heart, centre, stillness, and darkness. In *The Waves* the reader is aware of being controlled by the perceiving consciousness of the author; the poetic consciousness behind *Between the Acts* is more distanced. Here the reader is much more aware of the way in which language is being used: the obvious and deliberate exploitation of the variety of literary language in the literary pastiches of the Pageant, and the way in which the speech of the characters of the novel is shot through with bits of nursery rhymes, proverbs, or poetry that is usually misquoted. But apart from this, working at a deeper level and in a more complex way, there is the 'true' poetry which inheres in the rich verbal texture that reinforces the thematic framework of the novel, and which conveys meaning

THE 'PURE POETRY' OF *BETWEEN THE ACTS*

symbolically. Below the easy surface narrative, then, lies the darker layer of unease, insecurity, and instability, and this reflects, in the main, the mood of a nation on the verge of war. Behind this novel lies all the anguish that Virginia Woolf felt in the years leading up to the war and during the first years of the conflict.

Virginia Woolf and her husband believed that another European war would destroy western civilization completely. Leonard Woolf wrote in his autobiography:

If one was middle-aged or old and so had known at least a 'sort of kind' of civilization it was appalling impotently to watch the destruction of civilization by a powerful nation completely subservient to a gang of squalid, murderous hooligans.

(L. Woolf, *Downhill All the Way*: 254)

Virginia Woolf, on the other hand, writes about the war with the immediacy of experience:

"We have need of all our courage" are the words that come to the surface this morning: on hearing that all our windows are broken, ceilings down, and most of our china smashed at Mecklenburgh Square. The bomb exploded.... A grim morning.... As I say, we have need of courage. A very bad raid last night on London – waiting for the wireless. But I did forge ahead with P.H. [Pointz Hall, that is *Between the Acts*] all the same.

(18 September 1940; *AWD*: 352)

This extract from her diary is chosen not only for its content but also because of the difference in weighting between her long comment on the war and her brief reference to the book she is writing. There is no longer the elaborate explanation of her aims and techniques which is found, for example, when she is writing *The Years*. And this extract is characteristic of the distribution of emphasis on the whole in her diary during the war years.

Another kind of entry is that of 15 April 1939:

But considering how many things I have that I like – What's odd – (I'm always beginning like this) is the severance that war seems to bring: everything becomes meaningless: can't

VIRGINIA WOOLF AND THE POETRY OF FICTION

plan: then there comes too the community feeling: all England thinking the same thing – this horror of war – at the same moment. Never felt it so strong before. Then the lull and one lapses again into private separation.

(*AWD*: 313)

This particular kind of community feeling is something new in Virginia Woolf, and it comes through strongly in the remarks made by the crowd gathered at the Pageant in *Between the Acts*. And there, too, as the different acts finish, there is a lapse into 'private separation' to the tune of 'dispersed are we who have come together'. Some of the fragments of conversation that reach the ears of Miss La Trobe from the 'dispersed' crowd of the first interval are:

"No, I don't go by politicians. I've a friend who's been to Russia. He says... And my daughter, just back from Rome, she says the common people, in the cafés, hate Dictators...."

and

"And what about the Jews? The refugees... the Jews...."

(144–5)

During the second interval there is a change in mood and atmosphere. Here, much of what occurs or is said at a literal level expresses at the same time a more profound metaphoric meaning. Clouds gather overhead: literally the weather is unsettled, but so too is the audience, and snatches of conversation now work on several levels. Miss La Trobe's thoughts are anxious: 'Time was passing. How long would time hold them together? it was a gamble; a risk'(177). She is literally concerned about holding her audience together. But the next remark links back through this to the reference to the weather and gives to the whole sequence an ominous sense of the approaching catastrophe:

'It all looks very black.'
'No one wants it – save those damned Germans.'

(177)

In more ways than one, as one of the voices says, "The glass is falling"(178). The clouds of war are gathering. The outlook is black. There is a threat to what has been more or less stable

144

THE 'PURE POETRY' OF *BETWEEN THE ACTS*

for 500 years. This meaning is reinforced when the shower of rain comes later, in the lull before the audience is confronted by the mirrors. And here again the language suggests more than one level of meaning:

> And then the shower fell, sudden, profuse. No one had seen the cloud coming. There it was, black, swollen, on top of them. Down it poured like all the people in the world weeping. Tears. Tears. Tears.
>
> (210)

And when two drops of rain fell on Isa's face, 'They trickled down her cheeks as if they were her own tears. But they were all people's tears, weeping for all people.... The rain was sudden and universal'(210). As Mr Streatfield addresses the audience at the end of the Pageant distant music is heard:

> Twelve aeroplanes in perfect formation like a flight of wild duck came overhead. *That* was the music. The audience gaped; the audience gazed. Then zoom became drone. The planes had passed.
>
> (225)

In Pageant terms music is what unites. The new music seems to challenge them to unite to try to save and renew civilization.

The likely origin of the image of the wild duck in flight is suggested by a diary entry:

> Walking today (Nessa's birthday) by Kingfisher pool saw my first hospital train – laden, not funereal but weighty, as if not to shake bones.... Very quietly it slid into the cutting at Lewes. Instantly wild duck flights of aeroplanes came over head; manoeuvred; took up positions and passed over Caburn.
>
> (30 May 1940; *AWD*: 334)

Besides the immediacy of her response to the actuality of war Virginia Woolf also reflected deeply on the ethical and philosophical implications of war for humanity.

> What would war mean? Darkness, strain: I suppose conceivably death. And all the horror of friends: and Quentin:... All that lies over the water in the brain of that ridiculous little man. Why ridiculous? Because none of it

145

VIRGINIA WOOLF AND THE POETRY OF FICTION

fits: encloses no reality. Death and war and darkness representing nothing that any human being from the pork butcher to the Prime Minister cares one straw about. Not liberty, not life. Merely a housemaid's dream, and we woke from that dream and had the Cenotaph to remind us of the fruits. Well, I can't spread my mind wide enough to take it in, intelligibly. If it were real, one could make something of it. But as it is it merely grumbles, in an inarticulate way, behind reality. We may hear his mad voice vociferating tonight. Nuremberg rally begun.... And as we're all equally in the dark we can't cluster and group: we are beginning to feel the herd impulse: everyone asks everyone Any news? What d'you think? The only answer is Wait and see.

(5 September 1938; *A WD*: 301–2)

This personal record (and there are many more) of deeply felt anguish as one waited impotently for war to be declared underlies the symbolism of such phrases in *Between the Acts* as 'tears of the world', 'dumb yearning', and 'the universal moan'.

Between the Acts is, then, a poetic novel about a country and a people threatened by war. The time is June 1939. Yet actual references to the war are very few in number, and much of the kind of uncertainty and fear for the future that I have drawn attention to is embedded deeply below the surface of what is, in fact, a highly entertaining work.

It is just because of the novel's focus on the particular historical moment in which a country is about to go to war that certain expectations are raised in the reader's mind: it would seem reasonable to expect this novel to contain some of Virginia Woolf's most outspoken social and political comment. But this is not the case. That is to be found in her previous novel *The Years*; in *Between the Acts* the reader is presented with a way of life that seems old-fashioned and remote in its village setting and with its slower pace of life. The social scene of the 1930s in *The Years* is more intellectually 'modern' than that with which the reader is confronted in *Between the Acts*. This is surprising since what had been anticipated in the mid-1930s was closer to realization in 1939 and was actually happening when *Between the Acts* was published (1941). In *The Years*, for example, the vague 70-year-old Eleanor, who in many ways

146

THE 'PURE POETRY' OF *BETWEEN THE ACTS*

resembles Lucy Swithin, understands the nature of extreme authoritarianism and sees its threat in the form of Fascism to western civilization. This is revealed in her passionate response to seeing Mussolini's picture in a newspaper. In *Between the Acts*, on the other hand, Giles is angered by the way in which his whimsical aunt is completely out of touch with national and world events:

> Giles nicked his chair into position with a jerk. Thus only could he show his irritation, his rage with old fogies who sat and looked at views over coffee and cream when the whole of Europe – over there – was bristling like.... He had no command of metaphor. Only the ineffective word "hedgehog" illustrated his vision of Europe, bristling with guns, poised with planes.
>
> (66)

The reason why, on the face of it, *The Years* seems to give a more satisfying account of England in the dark days of the 1930s is because that novel is, in the main, a work of realism. What Virginia Woolf has to say about the state of the country is conveyed in a quite different way in *Between the Acts* because here she has returned to the poetic mode as a means of conveying her ideas, thoughts, and feelings. Instead of the more straightforward world of fact there is now the suggestive world of the metaphoric.

The whole of the surface of *Between the Acts*, the village, the country house, the church with its vicar and the church fund, is essentially metaphoric: it represents England and a form of Englishness that is immediately recognizable. All the nostalgia for a disappearing way of life, one that has gone on undisturbed for centuries, is embodied in that image of the village. It is the obvious stereotype of Little England.

The same image of peaceful English village life is examined in the 1911 section of *The Years*, and indeed that section of the novel seems to contain the germ of *Between the Acts*. It is interesting that Eleanor (she is 55 in 1911) thinks that that way of life would not be suitable for herself. She could not bear to become a grey-haired lady cutting flowers, tapping at cottage doors, and having the vicar to tea. And this image of what she could become suggests Lucy Swithin.

147

VIRGINIA WOOLF AND THE POETRY OF FICTION

Every summer Eleanor visits her brother Morris and his family at his mother-in-law's house in a Dorsetshire village, a house that resembles Pointz Hall. The Chinnerys (the family name of Morris's in-laws) had lived in the village since the beginning of time. Eleanor arrives late in the afternoon of the village bazaar which had been held in the grounds of the Chinnerys' house. There had been a play got up by a Miss Green. The proceeds of the bazaar are for the church fund. The village is threatened, Eleanor is told, by rich newcomers who want to build and who, it is feared, will alter the feel of the village and spoil the views. After dinner the family drink their coffee in the garden. As they sit in a semi-circle looking across the meadows at the fading hills Eleanor thinks to herself: 'This is England...' (*Y.* 223). And when they go indoors 'the drawing-room with its lamps lit had the effect of a stage' (*Y.* 224). All of this resembles the mood, setting, and action of *Between the Acts*. This, then, is England in 1911; and it is also England in 1939 when the Germans are ready for war.

Besides Pointz Hall and the village in general which represents England in *Between the Acts* there is the Pageant, which embodies 500 years of English history ending with the present time of the novel, June 1939. The Pageant begins with a small child saying 'England am I...' (94) and ends with 'Ourselves', the audience reflected in the mirrors, which represents the self as the culmination of history. In this way the two parts of the novel come together; through them Virginia Woolf builds up, respectively, her sense of history and her exploration of the human condition from within the individual consciousness, and finally integrates them in the present moment. Everything comes together in the novel to convey in a complex way her view of humanity at a particular historical moment. Pointz Hall and the Pageant are the two focal points of the novel. Yet it is in what Virginia Woolf does with them and how she works behind them that the real significance of the novel is to be found.

The literal exploration of the house called Pointz Hall, beginning with the drawing-room on the evening before the day of the Pageant and ending there twenty-four hours later when the Pageant is over, gives a simple outline to the more complex kind of structure set up thematically and also by the

148

THE 'PURE POETRY' OF *BETWEEN THE ACTS*

interplay of symbols and images that knit together the novel's two parts. With each description or presentation of a particular room or place, however, there is at the same time an inner exploration of either an individual consciousness or a relationship. The descriptive details, besides helping to create a vivid sense of place and a particular kind of atmosphere, often take on a meaning beyond the literal as the action of the novel develops. In this way the author's use of place becomes symbolic as well as structural.

The opening paragraph gives the book's setting and creates the mood. But the romantic suggestion of the opening words is at once undercut by reference to the cesspool: 'It was a summer's night and they were talking, in the big room with the windows open to the garden, about the cesspool'(7). Continually, throughout the novel, the gentler surface of village existence is subverted by hints of something darker below its surface. Reference to the cesspool's site then introduces the historical theme: it shows the remains, or more significantly 'scars', of the Britons, Romans, Elizabethans, and the period of the Napoleonic Wars. The people talking in the drawing-room are old Mr Oliver and his neighbours Mr and Mrs Haines. Then Mr Oliver's daughter-in-law Isa comes into the room wearing a faded dressing gown. She is silent, but through her stream of consciousness the reader learns that she is strongly attracted to Mr Haines whom she has met casually on two previous occasions. Mrs Haines is aware of the feeling that exists between her husband and Isa. Isa feels trapped in her marriage: '[she] was entangled, by her husband'(10).

The house itself is described in the early morning sunlight of the following day as 'middle-sized'. The bank above the house with its 'fringe of trees' forms part of the stage set provided by nature for Miss La Trobe's Pageant. The bank forms the terrace which old Bart Oliver tramps and along which the nurses wheel the perambulator. The inhabitants of this 'middle-sized' house are described as a 'middle-class' family. The next member of the house to be encountered is old Bart's sister, Lucy Swithin who has woken early because of the birdsong. To fill in the hours before breakfast she reads *An Outline of History* and thinks of

149

VIRGINIA WOOLF AND THE POETRY OF FICTION

rhododendron forests in Piccadilly; when the entire
continent, not then, she understood, divided by a channel,
was all one; populated, she understood, by elephant-bodied,
seal-necked, heaving, surging, slowly writhing, and, she
supposed, barking monsters; the iguanodon, the mammoth,
and the mastodon; from whom presumably, she thought,
jerking the window open, we descend.

(13)

Her reading of prehistory pushes the history theme further
back in time to the primitive life from which we descend and
which culminates in the final scene of the Pageant entitled
'Present time. Ourselves'. Reference to the time before
England was physically divided from the continent reflects
forwards to the present-day political division that will end in
war. Lucy draws curtains that are of faded white chintz, and
sits down to her morning tea surrounded by 'the usual trappings of rather shabby but gallant old age'(14-15). Here the
'faded' theme initiated in the reference to Isa's faded dressing
gown is picked up again.

From Lucy's bedroom the reader is then taken outdoors to
the terrace where the nurses are occupied with Isa's children.
Important here is the encounter between old Bart Oliver and
his young grandson George. The old man intrudes into and
shatters the beautiful imaginative world of the child, and then
distresses him further by the domineering way in which he
asserts his authority over his dog. Hitler, who is bent on
dominating other nations, is, of course, the 'great intruder'
who is feared in the summer of 1939. Old Bart is ruthlessly
authoritarian, asserting, however, that he is a man of reason
(he identifies with the 'Age of Reason' in the Pageant); the
child's world is a world of vision. The clash between the two
reflects emblematically the author's sense of the way in which
what is beautiful and fragile, or what belongs to 'civilization',
is vulnerable in the face of unimaginative force or power.

The child experiences a sense of unity or wholeness, something rarer and increasingly more difficult to achieve at the
end of the 1930s. Lucy Swithin believes in the possibility of
unity because of her religion and her imaginative flights of
what she calls 'one-making': 'Sheep, cows, grass, trees,

150

THE 'PURE POETRY' OF *BETWEEN THE ACTS*

ourselves – all are one.... we reach the conclusion that *all* is harmony, could we hear it. And we shall' (204). Miss La Trobe achieves it through art. Through the acts of the Pageant she unites audience and actors; in the interval they are 'dispersed' into the more habitual 'orts, scraps, and fragments'. Little George's sense of wholeness, however, is visionary. It is a 'moment of being' such as Virginia Woolf herself experienced as a small child in the garden of Talland House at St Ives – 'I was looking at a plant with a spread of leaves; and it seemed suddenly plain that the flower itself was a part of the earth; that a ring enclosed what was the flower; and that was the real flower; part earth; part flower' (*MB*: 71) – one of the 'moments' that is so significant in the conception of *The Waves*. And it is interesting that the language in which little George's experience is conveyed is on the whole more typical of *The Waves* than of *Between the Acts*.

The passage is one of poetic intensity:

> George grubbed. The flower blazed between the angles of the roots. Membrane after membrane was torn. It blazed a soft yellow, a lambent light under a film of velvet; it filled the caverns behind the eyes with light. All that inner darkness became a hall, leaf smelling, earth smelling of yellow light. And the tree was beyond the flower; the grass, the flower and the tree were entire.
>
> (16–17)

'Light' and 'fire' are constantly used by Virginia Woolf as symbols of life; and when combined with flowers they give an intensified impression of their life and beauty, as in, for instance, 'every flower seemed to burn by itself' (*MD*: 16). (The surrealist image of 'a match burning in a crocus' (*MD*: 36), conveys an experience of transcendence.) This is the immediate impression created by the simple statement: 'The flower blazed between the angles of the roots'. The ecstatic and visionary quality of the 'blazing' flower is controlled by the cold precision of its being placed 'between the angles of the roots'. The intensity is further modified and muted by a subtle use of oxymoron: 'It *blazed* a *soft* yellow, a *lambent* light...' (my italics). This seems to suggest that the fire of the flower's life or essence is below the surface, inside the

151

VIRGINIA WOOLF AND THE POETRY OF FICTION

beautiful exterior of the flower. The child can penetrate below that surface. The surface is functional as a kind of veil to the reality. This is implied through the word 'film' with its indistinct quality which combines with the sensuousness of 'velvet' to attract and to soothe.

There is then a sudden transference from the exterior world to the inner world of the child's perceiving consciousness: 'it filled the caverns behind the eyes with light. All that inner darkness became a hall, leaf smelling, earth smelling of yellow light'. The dark empty place within is filled and illumined, and the image of the whole inner hall illuminated and perfumed by wholesome earthy smells anticipates the description of the great barn. It is also the 'inner darkness' that triumphs at the end of the novel and which Giles and Isa reach through to, from which little George had been born, and from which 'another life might be born'(256). This poetic passage is, therefore, not an isolated incident but one that is locked imagistically into the whole text of the novel.

From the terrace the reader moves indoors again to encounter Isa in her bedroom. There is, however, a link between the two locations as the nurses with the children move into Isa's line of vision. Isa taps on the window to attract their attention but they do not notice her. Her attempt to communicate with them is, in other words, abortive. This introduces the 'abortive' theme which, as it is used by Virginia Woolf, is a theme of failure or lack of fulfilment, indicating usually that the promise or possibility of development had been there but had not come to realization. The theme is most obviously embodied in the person of Isa:

> "Abortive," was the word that expressed her. She never came out of a shop, for example, with the clothes she admired; nor did her figure, seen against the dark roll of trousering in a shop window, please her. Thick of waist, large of limb, and, save for her hair, fashionable in the tight modern way, she never looked like Sappho, or one of the beautiful young men whose photographs adorned the weekly papers.
>
> (21–2)

The trivial details listed here are indicative of a definite personality, one that is indecisive, unsure of herself and feels

THE 'PURE POETRY' OF *BETWEEN THE ACTS*

less physically attractive than she might be. More significantly, there are 'abortive' aspects to her relationship with her husband Giles and to her desire for Rupert Haines. She habitually refers to the former as 'the father of my children', and she fails to gain the attention of the latter who obviously rouses stronger feelings in her. The reference to Sappho and to 'young men' suggests another 'abortive' aspect. Isa attempts, not very successfully, to write poetry: 'The words weren't worth writing in the book bound like an account book in case Giles suspected'(21). Here, with economy, Virginia Woolf indicates at the same time Isa's inability to share something she cares deeply about with her husband. Isa sees all this, her 'abortive' life, when she looks into the mirror on her dressing-table.

The 'mirror' is referred to again, but as a cliché, in the library section that comes next. ' "Books are the mirrors of the soul." ' A foolish, flattering lady had once said this, adding too that the library was ' "the heart of the house" '(22). And the narrative voice says that the village is in 'the very heart of England'. In this way the 'mirror' theme which culminates in the final scene of the Pageant when the audience is confronted by mirrors, and the 'heart' or 'centre' theme which culminates in the 'heart of darkness' at the end of the novel, are being gradually built up. Old Bart enters the empty room, sits in his chair with his dog at his feet and falls asleep. His life, mostly past now, is 'mirrored' in his dreams: 'But the master was not dead; only dreaming; drowsily, seeing as in a glass, its lustre spotted, himself, a young man helmeted; and a cascade falling'(24). Isa, coming into the library, 'intrudes' into his dreams:

"Am I," Isa apologised, "interrupting?"
Of course she was – destroying youth and India.

(24)

Looking around Isa repeats the remark that books are the 'mirror of the soul' but goes on to question the validity of books for her generation: 'What remedy was there for her at her age – the age of the century, thirty-nine – in books? Book-shy she was, like the rest of her generation; and gun-shy too'(26). As she glances at different titles she suggests that a 'cure' for the aches of the people of her day and age might be

153

VIRGINIA WOOLF AND THE POETRY OF FICTION

found in 'perhaps not a person's life; a country's' (26). The real end of her search might well be the Pageant which is her country's life. She comes to the conclusion, however, that 'For her generation the newspaper was a book'(26). She then picks up *The Times* and reads of the rape of a girl by troopers in the barracks at Whitehall. Her stream of consciousness reveals a sense of dissatisfaction and an awareness of the violence in life, and above all, a feeling that life is precarious and that old answers and remedies will not do for the needs and ills of her generation or for the dangers that beset the country in 1939. The undercurrent of horror at the prospect of war is fore-grounded in Isa's reflections, but the surface existence goes on. Lucy comes in, the Pageant is discussed, and the tone lightens again.

When Lucy Swithin comes into the library attention focuses on the brother-sister relationship and talk turns to preparations for the Pageant. Old Bart belongs to the world of fact, Lucy to the world of vision. He ridicules the things she believes in, she fears the harshness of his censure. All her life he has assumed an attitude of superiority and dominated her. This is economically and suggestively conveyed by the word 'sidling' which describes the way in which she walks past her brother to replace a hammer in the cupboard. The same word had been used to describe the way in which Sohrab the Afghan hound had moved in response to the old man's commands:

> Back came the Afghan hound, sidling, apologetic. And as he cringed at the old man's feet, a string was slipped over his collar; the noose that old Oliver always carried with him.
>
> (18)

It was this manifestation of control over the animal that had caused little George to cry.

Lucy had been nailing a placard to the barn. Talk then turns naturally to the Pageant and the weather. From the library Lucy goes to the kitchen where she and Mrs Sands make sandwiches for the tea-interval. Lucy takes them to the barn. Preparations for lunch are under way. Things are speeding up and there is a sense of anticipation in the air. A message comes that Giles will be late for lunch. He is

THE 'PURE POETRY' OF *BETWEEN THE ACTS*

obviously returning from London in the middle of the day because of the Pageant.

The dining-room lies across the hall from the library. After checking that all is in order for lunch the butler goes out of the room. There follows a set-piece description of the empty room which culminates in the kind of 'pure' poetry I referred to earlier. Two pictures hang on the wall facing the window, the one of a man, the other of a woman. The man is an ancestor who was fond of his horse and his dog. The woman is an unknown lady. The ancestor's wish to have his dog buried at his feet had not been granted. Here, imagistically, a link is made between old Bart and the man in the picture. Old Bart's Afghan hound often assumes the position and attitude of a faithful dog at his master's feet. In the library episode, for instance, the crusader-dog image makes the idea explicit:

> [He] sank down into the chintz-covered chair with the dog at his feet – the Afghan hound. His nose on his paws, his haunches drawn up, he looked a stone dog, a crusader's dog, guarding even in the realms of death the sleep of his master. But the master was not dead....
>
> (23–4)

This picture is a 'talk producer': the way in which it does produce talk is demonstrated in the lunch scene as old Bart makes social conversation to entertain his guests. The picture is also in some measure a symbolic representation of old Bart himself. The picture of the lady, on the other hand, leads into silence, and is representative of Lucy Swithin. The mannerist painting of the lady, with her silver arrow and a feather in her hair, suggests Diana. And the Diana figure suggests Lucy. Old Bart is often amazed by her chaste aspect, as when he reflects: 'How, he wondered, had she ever borne children?' (140). The silent lady presides over the silent empty room which is then poetically celebrated:

> Empty, empty, empty; silent, silent, silent. The room was a shell, singing of what was before time was; a vase stood in the heart of the house, alabaster, smooth, cold, holding the still, distilled essence of emptiness, silence.
>
> (47)

155

VIRGINIA WOOLF AND THE POETRY OF FICTION

This kind of 'poetry' is something quite new in Virginia Woolf's fiction; it is more essentially 'verbal', by which I mean that the poetry is created as much by the play and pattern of words as in the functional use of imagery. 'Silence', 'heart', and 'time' are significant key and theme words in the novel. Their being brought together here and almost isolated from character and incident makes this passage a kind of abstract of the novel.

The passage begins with the fact and concrete detail of the empty silent room, and then metaphor is introduced ('the room was a shell...') which transcends the factual meaning. When a shell is held to the ear the sound of the sea is heard. The sea, or water, is an archetypal image of life. What is heard in the shell of the room, therefore, is something eternal; something of 'what was before time was'. But the sense of the shell as a bare and empty framework of a room or house seems also to be intended since that is the meaning it is given at the end of the novel when the members of the Pointz Hall family experience individually a moment of fruitful silence in which place, event, and life are laid bare for them: 'Within the shell of the room she overlooked the summer night'(250). 'Isa had done with her bills. Sitting in the shell of the room she watched the pageant fade'(252). Finally, a vase in the dining-room is described. The substance it is made of and the qualities of that substance are indicated, but the shape of the vase is not given. Its contents are symbolic.

In this brief poetic passage a process of abstraction and distillation is gone through. The movement is from the literal (an empty and silent room) to the abstract (emptiness, silence) and finally to the essential (distilled essence).

With the conclusion of this brief descriptive section Bart, Lucy, and Isa emerge from the library; as they move towards the dining-room they encounter Mrs Manresa and William Dodge. The house has not yet been completely explored. There remain the nursery and one or two bedrooms. (These are visited later when Lucy takes William Dodge on a tour of the house.) But the chief members of the family have been met. Their private thoughts, feelings, and preoccupations have been revealed and their relationships established. The Pointz Hall family as a family unit, in other words, has been carefully built up from knowledge of the individual from within his or her

156

THE 'PURE POETRY' OF *BETWEEN THE ACTS*

own consciousness, to an understanding of each's relation to the other within that family group. Important themes have been introduced, some embodied in individual characters such as the theme of dominance and intrusion in old Bart or the 'abortive' theme in Isa Oliver, whereas the social themes and the theme of history emerge from the group as a whole, in their activity as well as from their thoughts and feelings. Literal places like the lily pond and the barn have been noted; these take on symbolic significance in the course of the novel. With the 'intrusion' of Mrs Manresa and William Dodge, the Pointz Hall section proper seems to close. As old Bart has observed: 'The family was not a family in the presence of strangers'(61).

The shift from Pointz Hall to the Pageant is made gradually, beginning when the Olivers and their guests go into the garden after lunch. They sit drinking their coffee within earshot of Miss La Trobe and the actors who are getting ready for the Pageant. When Mrs Manresa notices their sound – ' "Don't I hear?" She listened. She heard laughter, down among the bushes, where the terrace dipped to the bushes'(70) – a definite link is being formed between the two sets of people representing respectively Pointz Hall and the Pageant, and the authorial narrative oscillates between the two until they all come together at the actual Pageant. Here Virginia Woolf is creating a kind of Chinese boxes structure, as she does through the 'centre' and 'heart' image (the library is the heart of the house; the house is central to the village; the village is in the heart of England). Miss La Trobe comes to the grounds of Pointz Hall; the Olivers emerge from the house to see the Pageant that is put in their grounds; as they become absorbed by the Pageant they find themselves at its centre. In this way the two parts of *Between the Acts* become interlocked.

The Pageant begins with a child saying 'England am I' (94) and ends with the National Anthem. It is a celebration of England and Englishness through its representation of English history. It falls into two interacting sections, the 'Acts' and the intervals between them which are largely controlled by what occurs during the acts. The interaction between acts and intervals embodies the unity–separation theme of the novel. It is the responsibility of Miss La Trobe to draw the audience out

157

VIRGINIA WOOLF AND THE POETRY OF FICTION

of its separateness and music is her means of initiating the process of unification. This is first observed as the flamboyant Mrs Manresa is drawn into the performance:

> She was afloat on the stream of the melody. Radiating royalty, complacency, good humour, the wild child was Queen of the festival. The play had begun.
>
> (97)

Each of the novel's main characters is drawn out of his or her own sense of isolation by a specific moment or act of the play. Mrs Manresa identifies herself with the Elizabethan age. Isa is arrested by the words of an Elizabethan tragedy. William Dodge responds enthusiastically to the visual effectiveness and movement of the whole company round Queen Elizabeth: 'An entrancing spectacle (to William) of dappled light and shade on half-clothed, fantastically coloured, leaping, jerking, swinging legs and arms'(112). These three have found something that has touched them personally in Act I. As the Elizabethan Age passes from the stage at the end of the act the 'Between-the-Acts' theme words are heard: the audience disperses for the interval to the tune of 'Dispersed are we'(125).

Although there is much surface activity during the interval as people make their way to the barn for refreshments, a significant layer of individual psychological experience is also indicated, often in the language of, or in metaphors drawn from, the Pageant or from the theatre generally. The effect of this is to blur the edges between the actor/audience, real/fictional, Pointz Hall/Pageant polarities. Feeling frustrated and lonely because she cannot see Rupert Haines, Isa, for instance, hums to Miss La Trobe's melancholy tune of dispersal: ' "All is over. The wave has broken.... Single, separate on the shingle" '(115).

Mrs Manresa's response to Giles as he enters the barn and she notices the blood on his shoes is expressed in terms of acting out roles in a play:

> Vaguely some sense that he had proved his valour for her admiration flattered her. If vague it was sweet. Taking him in tow, she felt: I am the Queen, he my hero, my sulky hero.
>
> (128)

158

THE 'PURE POETRY' OF *BETWEEN THE ACTS*

In responding to her Giles is momentarily drawn out of his separateness. This is expressed in terms of the Pageant but in a slightly different way. She releases him from his burden of being an onlooker:

> And she was a thorough good sort, making him feel less of an audience, more of an actor, going round the Barn in her wake.

(129)

Isa's response to Giles is very different from what she feels when her small son runs towards her. This is conveyed metaphorically as a costume change: William Dodge 'saw her face change, as if she had got out of one dress and put on another'(126). As she turns from the child and catches a glimpse of her husband, William Dodge notes: 'Then again she changed her dress. This time, from the expression in her eyes it was apparently something in the nature of a strait waistcoat'(126).

These individual responses reveal something of the central relationships of the novel. Between Isa, Giles, Mrs Manresa, and William three conflicting pairings take place. Giles affects Isa and William Dodge simultaneously. Isa at his approach is torn between love and hate. William Dodge is roused by Giles. Giles, however, recognizing that he is a homosexual, despises him. Giles is jealously trying to find out who it is that his wife is interested in, sensing that he is somewhere in the Barn. Isa, looking for Rupert Haines, never finds him. Mrs Manresa is after Giles who is not indifferent to her: they walk across the lawn together at the end of the interval. Old Bart also responds to the fulsomeness of Mrs Manresa: she 'stirs the stagnant pool of his old heart'(142). Evident in these relations is a disturbing sense of general sexual frustration.

All these people are, however, rescued from their uneasy sense of separateness when the Pageant is resumed. When they return to their seats for the Second Act music once again sets the unifying process in motion: 'Miss La Trobe watched them sink down peacefully into the nursery rhyme'(146). The Second Act is the Age of Reason, and its lively parody of eighteenth-century literary forms and styles captivates old Bart Oliver. As he is symbolically caught up in the action on stage

VIRGINIA WOOLF AND THE POETRY OF FICTION

he relinquishes his more habitual role of being a 'separatist': 'Old Bartholomew applauded. "Hear! Hear!" he cried. "Bravo! Bravo!" Thus encouraged Reason spoke out'(146–7). For some time 'Reason held the centre of the stage alone'(148). By the end of the first scene of the Restoration Comedy called *Where There's a Will There's a Way* old Bart is beginning to adopt the speech of the play:

> "Reason, begad! Reason!" exclaimed old Bartholomew, and looked at his son as if exhorting him to give over these womanish vapours and be a man, Sir.
>
> (157)

And by the end of the play he has identified himself with the Age of Reason. He has taken on its thought and speech:

> "God's truth!" cried Bartholomew catching the infection of the language. "There's a moral for you!"
> He threw himself back in his chair and laughed, like a horse whinnying.
>
> (174)

The other separatist, his son Giles, is similarly influenced by the Age of Reason. The play's title touches him on the raw: figuratively the words 'rose and pointed a finger of scorn at him'(174–5). He responds as if he were acting out the hero's part

> Off to Gretna Green with his girl; the deed done. Damn the consequences.
> "Like to see the greenhouse?" he said abruptly, turning to Mrs. Manresa.
> "Love to!" she exclaimed, and rose.
>
> (175)

The mood of the interval that follows the Age of Reason is more sombre. There are signs that all have been touched by the Pageant. Something in the play has unsettled and disturbed them:

> Yet somehow they felt – how could one put it – a little not quite here or there. As if the play had jerked the ball out of the cup; as if what I call myself was still floating unattached, and didn't settle. Not quite themselves, they felt.
>
> (175)

160

THE 'PURE POETRY' OF *BETWEEN THE ACTS*

Individuals, as we have already noted, are disturbed by what is happening in Germany: ' "It all looks very black" '(177). The sense of being 'unsettled' works at several levels. The weather, too, becomes suddenly unsettled. And Miss La Trobe's anxiety about her ability to unite her audience has undertones of social and political unease: 'Time was passing. How long would time hold them together? It was a gamble; a risk'(177). As each scene moves forward in time and closer, therefore, to the present, hints of anxiety about the contemporary state of the nation are more in evidence.

The nineteenth-century scenes enact such Victorian stereo-types as Authority, Piety, and a sense of Empire. Colonel Mayhew notes with surprise, however, that the British Army is not included. Because the Victorians are closest in time to the present they touch the audience personally. ' "Were they like that?" ' Isa asks. Her aunt who has actually lived during Queen Victoria's reign replies with one of her sideways comments that reveals a profound perception of the nature of history, of human nature, and the significance of time and social change:

"The Victorians," Mrs. Swithin mused. "I don't believe"
she said with her odd little smile, "that there ever were such
people. Only you and me and William dressed differently."

(203)

Lucy Swithin explicitly dissolves the distinction between past and present, thus asserting the essential unity of history. This perception adds a further dimension to her spatial 'one-making'. Similarly Miss La Trobe points to the unity of history when she confronts her audience with the mirrors: the present is the continuation of the past; we 'ourselves' are the summa-tion of history.

The novel which begins with Pointz Hall moves outwards to the Pageant. After the Pageant there is a return to Pointz Hall. With the departure of the audience Virginia Woolf makes one of those technically perfect arrangements of passages: 'The little company who had come together at luncheon were left standing on the terrace'(235). The sequence of groupings that forms the return to Pointz Hall is a retracing of the sequence that was formed in moving from Pointz Hall to the

VIRGINIA WOOLF AND THE POETRY OF FICTION

Pageant. The 'little company' of the Olivers and their guests is again alone on the terrace. Then Mrs Manresa and William Dodge leave, and the family becomes a family again. Below the surface a more profound transition is effected. What has been seen and experienced in the Pageant has been absorbed and taken away from it in much the same way that the Highland reaper's song remained with Wordsworth when the singing was over:

> And as I mounted up the hill,
> The music in my heart I bore,
> Long after it was heard no more.
>
> (*The Solitary Reaper*)

A definite hope that this would occur is expressed in a qualifying remark added to the gramophone's valediction:

> *Dispersed are we, who have come together.* But, the gramophone asserted, *let us retain whatever made that harmony.*
>
> (229)

In the final section of the novel the family is indoors. The wheel has come full circle. A new beginning is found creatively and symbolically in the 'heart of darkness'. After the old people have retired for the night Giles and Isa find each other again in the darkness. Life and the primeval passions are laid bare:

> Before they slept, they must fight; after they had fought, they would embrace. From that embrace another life might be born. But first they must fight, as the dog fox fights with the vixen, in the heart of darkness, in the fields of night.
>
> (255-6)

The continuance and rebirth of life is paralleled by the continuance and rebirth of art: Miss La Trobe conceives a new play as she drinks her whisky and soda in the pub:

> Words of one syllable sank down into the mud.... The mud became fertile. Words rose above the intolerably laden dumb oxen plodding through the mud. Words without meaning – wonderful words.
>
> (247-8)

162

THE 'PURE POETRY' OF *BETWEEN THE ACTS*

The possibility of a new life being born, a new play conceived, gives a sense of life and optimism to the novel despite many of its dark undertones. The symbolic Pageant goes on. Little England will grow up. The struggle to communicate and achieve unity is re-enacted in the novel's conclusion. The true experience of the Pageant, the reality that will live on or be found again by members of the audience in their own private lives, is suggested by the authorial narration of a parable of music at the end of the Pageant:

> The whole population of the mind's immeasurable profundity came flocking; from the unprotected, the unskinned; and dawn rose; and azure; from chaos and cacophony measure; but not the melody of surface sound alone controlled it; but also the warring battle-plumed warriors straining asunder: To part? No. Compelled from the ends of the horizon; recalled from the edge of appalling crevasses; they crashed; solved; united.
>
> (220–1)

The poetic undercurrent below the surface 'action' of Pointz Hall and the Pageant has already been detected in a few recurring symbols or words of symbolic implication such as mirror, heart or centre, silent, and so on. They have been noted contextually but, with the exception of the word 'silence' which develops into the poem of silence in the dining-room section of Pointz Hall, their coherence and patterning which locks the thematic into the wider structural framework of the novel has not yet been explored. It is this kind of coherence and patterning that creates what I referred to earlier as the 'pure' poetry of *Between the Acts*. It is, therefore, in that third layer of meaning below the novel's overall image of the village as England, below the symbolic embodiment of meaning in the interlocked Pointz Hall–Pageant areas of interest, that the poetic core of the novel is to be found.

Certain of the novel's themes are built up through recurrent theme words such as silent or heart while others are embodied primarily in symbols such as the mirror, or through repeated reference to symbolic places like the lily pool which has a wide and complex web of meaning attached to it.

163

VIRGINIA WOOLF AND THE POETRY OF FICTION

The symbol of the mirror, as we have seen, is introduced when Isa sits at her dressing-table mirror. Three versions of her face are reflected back to her from the 'three-fold' mirror. When she looks into her eyes they reflect back to her, her passionate feeling for Rupert Haines. This instance is parodied in the Restoration drama that is central to the Age of Reason section of the Pageant: Lady Harpy Harraden is in her dressing-room.

Lady H.H. (gazing in the glass) *So, so – what was it? Some silly trash! Cupid's dart – hah, hah! lighting his taper – tush – at my eyes ... pooh!*

(150)

The mirror symbolically gives rise to a multiplicity of meanings in the library section of the Pointz Hall part of the novel: books reflect the soul, the dreams of old age reflect youthful vigour and excitement, newspapers reflect modern reality. The climax of the mirror or reflection theme and the recurring use of the mirror symbol comes dramatically at the end of the Pageant. In the brief pause before the final scene there is a sense of unease as the audience sits waiting to see 'Present time. Ourselves'(206). Apart from the reflection of present day on stage in the emblematic scene of the man with a hod on his back building the wall of civilization, there is the literal reflection of the present when children carrying mirrors mingle with the audience. Those who are caught by the mirrors feel discomfort and resentment; those watching them are amused. Then after a finale the mirror-bearers come on stage; they stand still, thus compelling all the members of the audience to see themselves. There is a pause in time dramatically and symbolically:

The hands of the clock had stopped at the present moment. It was now. Ourselves.
So that was her little game! To show us up, as we are, here and now. All shifted, preened, minced; hands were raised, legs shifted. Even Bart, even Lucy, turned away. All evaded or shaded themselves – save Mrs. Manresa who, facing herself in the glass, used it as a glass; had out her mirror;

164

THE 'PURE POETRY' OF *BETWEEN THE ACTS*

powdered her nose; and moved one curl, disturbed by the breeze, to its place.

(216–17)

Mrs Manresa, by virtue of her make-up – less natural-looking at the end of the day: 'plated it looked, not deeply inter-fused' (236) – has provided herself with a protective layer which conceals from others the reality of her true self. Thus, unlike the others, she does not flinch when confronted by the image in the mirror. The rest try to escape: ' "The play's over, I take it," muttered Colonel Mayhew, retrieving his hat. "It's time..." ' (217). But to prevent an immediate retreat an anony-mous voice from the bushes comments on the significance of the looking-glasses:

> *Let's break the rhythm and forget the rhyme. And calmly consider ourselves. Ourselves. Some bony. Some fat.* (The glasses confirmed this.) *Liars most of us. Thieves too.* (The glasses made no comment on that.)
>
> (218)

As the voice goes through the variety of individual reflections the emphasis shifts to a comment that it is out of such 'orts, scraps and fragments' as we 'ourselves' are that the wall of civilization is built. So the individual is locked into civilization. We are civilization; the individual is part of the evolving historical process. By the time the audience finally disperses after the vicar's inept and embarrassing attempt to interpret the Pageant the intensity of feeling caused by the confrontation with the mirrors is dispelled. The incident quietly falls into place in the perspecive of the whole:

> Rather a cracked old bell ... And the mirrors! Reflecting us... I called that cruel. One feels such a fool, caught unprotected... There's Mr. Streatfield, going, I suppose to take the evening service.
>
> (233)

Unlike the mirror theme, which as a concrete object becomes a symbolic metaphor (books as the mirror of the soul) until finally real mirrors produce a symbolic reflection of the self at the

165

VIRGINIA WOOLF AND THE POETRY OF FICTION

end of the Pageant, the theme of silence is built up through a repetition of the words 'silent', 'silence', or 'silently' and in the function of silence as an activity. During lunch Isa takes on the role of being the silent figure. Virginia Woolf uses her silence to penetrate below the social surface of the group sitting round the table. In this way Mrs Manresa is presented to the reader through Isa's consciousness:

> "Or what are your rings for, and your nails, and that really adorable little straw hat?" said Isabella addressing Mrs. Manresa silently and thereby making silence add its unmistakable contribution to talk.

> (49–50)

Similarly she had weighed up William Dodge on his arrival:

> In all this sound of welcome, protestation, apology and again welcome, there was an element of silence supplied by Isabella, observing the unknown young man. He was of course a gentleman; witness socks and trousers; brainy – tie spotted, waistcoat undone....

> (48–9)

As lunch proceeds William Dodge is labelled the silent guest (67), and when old Bart makes an effort to draw him out of his silence he escapes into the picture of the silent lady: 'The picture drew them down the paths of silence'(57).

Apart from this kind of penetrative silence, silence is also explored by Virginia Woolf as a condition of isolation and as a feature of social or personal defeat. Giles, for example, remains silent before his aunt who angers him because of what she is:

> "And what did you think of the play?" she [Mrs. Manresa] asked.
>
> Bartholomew looked at his son. His son remained silent.
>
> "And you Mrs. Swithin?" Mrs. Manresa pressed the old lady...
>
> No one answered.
>
> "Look!" Lucy exclaimed.
>
> "The birds?" said Mrs. Manresa, looking up.
>
> There was a bird with a straw in its beak; and the straw dropped.

THE 'PURE POETRY' OF *BETWEEN THE ACTS*

Lucy clapped her hands. Giles turned away.

(130–1)

There is, moreover, a burden of silence that all must at times bear. This is felt, for instance, when the Olivers and their guests are sitting together in the garden but do not feel united as a group.

They were silent. They stared at the view, as if something might happen in one of those fields to relieve them of the intolerable burden of sitting silent, doing nothing, in company.

(81)

Virginia Woolf resorts to the pathetic fallacy to intensify the oppressive nature of the experience. Nature, too, bears the burden: 'The view laid bare by the sun was flattened, silenced, stilled'(81).

Finally, the silence theme is condensed into two poetic passages which, in their different kinds of poetry, convey respectively the abstraction of silence and its human embodiment. The former (the vase of silence) has already been considered. The latter is found in a miniature character study of Bond the cowman:

He contemplated the young people hanging roses from one rafter to another. He thought very little of anybody, simples or gentry. Leaning, silent, sardonic, against the door he was like a withered willow, bent over a stream, all its leaves shed, and in his eyes the whimsical flow of the waters.

(36)

Bond's silence places him outside the world of the young villagers who are decorating the barn. It provides him with a rich inner life of beauty and sadness. The 'flow of the waters' is an archetypal symbol of life; the epithet 'whimsical' indicates his particular vision of life. As these 'waters' are reflected in his eyes the outer becomes the inner much as the external beauty discovered by little George in a flower reached within to fill the caverns behind his eyes. It is in her heightened use of language that Virginia Woolf is able in this way to

VIRGINIA WOOLF AND THE POETRY OF FICTION

transmute the outer landscape into a landscape of the mind
and to reach by means of a concrete outer object to an inner
meaning or even to a visionary experience. The power of this
passage lies in its complete fusion of image and meaning: the
image of the willow by the stream is so fused with the cowman
at the barn that what is said of the one has resonances for the
other, but the two cannot be separated out.

Isolating key words and symbols for close scrutiny in this
way at once reveals the kind of close verbal structure that
underpins the lighthearted easy-flowing surface narrative of
the novel. Even more remarkable is the way in which such
words interlock with each other to create an even greater
density in the writing. There is constant interplay between
themes and the words of symbolic content that embody them,
especially between those of mirror/reflection, the centre or
heart (examined in discussing the library section of the novel),
and silence. The vase of silence, for instance, stands in the
heart of the house. The fish in the lily pool manoeuvre their
way silently above 'a black cushion of mud'; it is in that 'deep
centre, in that black heart' (54–5), the legend goes, that a lady
drowned herself. The picture of the lady in the dining-room
leads into the 'heart of silence' (63). At the end of the day,
after Lucy and old Bart have retired for the night Giles and Isa
sit alone together in silence; then they move into the 'heart of
darkness' (256). It is this kind of resonating verbal interplay
that comes close to what Mallarmé means by 'pure' poetry: 'If
the poem is to be pure ... the initiative [must be] taken by the
words themselves, which will be set in motion as they meet
unequally in collision.' It is their 'exchange of gleams' that
produces meaning and beauty (Mallarmé, 'Crisis in Poetry':
40–1).

Another related way in which Virginia Woolf creates this
kind of 'pure' poetry is through her symbolic use of place.
One such place is the medieval barn in the grounds of Pointz
Hall; another is the lily pool that can be seen from the dining-
room window of the Hall.

The barn is first alluded to as the place where Lucy has
nailed her placard, and the first poetic description of it occurs
in a fairly factual and humorous account of her activity:

THE 'PURE POETRY' OF *BETWEEN THE ACTS*

It was as old as the church, and built of the same stone, but
it had no steeple. It was raised on cones of grey stone at the
corners to protect it from rats and damp. Those who had
been to Greece always said it reminded them of a temple.
Those who had never been to Greece – the majority –
admired it all the same. The roof was weathered red-orange;
and inside it was a hollow hall, sun-shafted, brown, smelling
of corn, dark when the doors were shut, but splendidly
illuminated when the doors at the end stood open, as they
did to let the wagons in – the long low wagons, like ships of
the sea, breasting the corn, not the sea, returning in the
evening shagged with hay. The lanes caught tufts where the
wagons had passed.

(34)

Comparisons, both explicit and implicit, with the church are
significant. Both are made of the same stone and are of the
same age. The barn looks like a place of worship. It is
'splendidly illuminated' naturally whereas the church requires
artificial lighting (the proceeds of the Pageant are for the
installation of electric light). It is full of life and warmth
whereas church congregations are falling off.

The heightened poetic moment of the passage is built round
the image of the harbour or haven and the homecoming of
laden ships. The imaging of the corn as sea is done with
economy of language in the phrase 'breasting the corn'. The
very feel and texture of the corn is conveyed onomatopoeically
in the words 'tufts' and 'shagged'. The sense of ships or
wagons returning in the evening parallels the return home of
the people after the Pageant.

The barn, too, has a kind of all-purpose quality. If it rains
the Pageant can be acted in it. Refreshments are served there
during the interval. It is in the tea interval that the second
description of the barn is found. Here there is an apostrophe
to the barn in which details from the earlier description are
repeated. The summary of the earlier passage is almost a
parenthesis within the simple statement: 'The Barn ... was
empty':

The Barn, the Noble Barn, the barn that had been built
over seven hundred years ago and reminded some people of

169

a Greek temple, others of the middle ages, most people of an age before their own, scarcely anybody of the present moment, was empty.

(119)

Waiting for the crowd to arrive, Virginia Woolf extends the earlier description to include its animal and insect life. Here a variety of small creatures find shelter and food. The vividness and liveliness of the scene is created largely through the simple use of verbs that suggest activity: 'Mice slid in and out of holes...'(119); 'Countless beetles and insects of various sorts burrowed in the dry wood'(120). This kind of life is carried on in all areas of the barn including the rafters. The idyllic description of the natural life of the barn is then linked with the human life associated with it in an imaginative sense of the comic. Disney-like, 'A blue-bottle had settled on the cake and stabbed its yellow rock with its short drill'(120). All the beauty and warmth is then momentarily negated as the barn is viewed through the eyes of the unimaginative cook: 'mice were only black pellets in kitchen drawers; moths she bundled in her hands and put out of the window'(120).

Finally, much of what has been stated about the barn is now enacted. The barn is admired, for instance: ' "This fine old Barn..." said Mrs. Manresa, stopping in the doorway'(121). It then becomes full of people. As if to bring this second description of the barn to completion an image from the earlier description is picked up: a different kind of ship comes into harbour as Mrs Manresa enters the barn with her 'merchandise'. She takes Giles 'in tow'(128); he goes through the barn 'in her wake'(129).

Virginia Woolf's treatment of the barn as a symbol is different in kind from her handling of other symbols such as the mirror or key words such as 'silent'. The word 'silent' and the symbol of the mirror recur throughout *Between the Acts* to create the themes of silence and reflection and to draw together allusively different moments in the book, thus building up a structure of meaning and of imagery. References to the barn, on the other hand, do not recur in the same kind of way. The symbolism of the barn spans the book as a whole, but it is from these two focal descriptions of it, in which an

170

THE 'PURE POETRY' OF *BETWEEN THE ACTS*

appreciation for certain values has been established, that it does so.

Two different techniques are combined in creating the symbolism of the lily pool. There is a long poetic description of the pool like the long poetic description of the barn. In addition to this, however, there are several recurring references to the pool which make this a symbolic place of even greater scale and scope. The first description is a fairly straightforward account of the pool with the scullery maid standing beside it, and it occurs in the first Pointz Hall section of the novel, before, that is, the performance of the Pageant. The second, and much more symbolic passage comes after the Pageant when old Bart and his sister Lucy are standing by it. Many descriptive details from the first passage that recur throughout the novel gathering significance are brought together in the later passage which is thereby enriched with an accumulation of meaning, implication, and symbolism. In the first passage the pool is described as a background to the maid who has come out to cool her cheeks:

> There had always been lilies there, self-sown from wind-dropped seed, floating red and white on the green plates of their leaves. Water, for hundreds of years, had silted down into the hollow, and lay there four or five feet deep over a black cushion of mud. Under the thick plate of green water, glazed in their self-centred world, fish swam – gold, splashed with white, streaked with black or silver. Silently they manoeuvred in their water world, poised in the blue patch made by the sky, or shot silently to the edge where the grass, trembling, made a fringe of nodding shadow. On the water-pavement spiders printed their delicate feet. A grain fell and spiralled down; a petal fell, filled and sank. At that the fleet of boat-shaped bodies paused; poised; equipped; mailed; then with a waver of undulation off they flashed.
>
> It was in that deep centre, in that black heart, that the lady had drowned herself.... But, the servants insisted, they must have a ghost; the ghost must be a lady's; who had drowned herself for love.

(54–5)

171

VIRGINIA WOOLF AND THE POETRY OF FICTION

The pool has grown and developed through the natural process of time. The 'plate' image referring first to the waterlily leaves is extended to refer to the pool itself (the thick plate of green water). It draws attention to the surface of the water. From this there develops naturally a distinction between what is of the surface and what is below it, which leads naturally to the implications of the theme of appearance and reality. The black mud, or the 'black heart', of the pool takes on many meanings in the course of the novel. The second paragraph focuses on the legend of the drowned lady with its accompanying superstition of the 'ghost'.

The pool is accurately placed geographically in a position between the house and the place where the Pageant is performed. It is also interesting compositionally that the first description of it is given between the first Pointz Hall section of the book and the Pageant and the second between the pageant and the final Pointz Hall section. Both geographically and structurally, therefore, the lily pool which is found between the house and the Pageant is a 'central' place.

The second pool passage differs from the first by not being a continuous passage of descriptive writing. It is a kind of broken up and extended symbolic reference to the pool. After the Pageant old Bart stands by the pool and is then joined by his sister who asks him if they should thank Miss La Trobe. The thoughts and feelings of brother and sister are then presented figuratively as Virginia Woolf draws metaphor and symbol from details of the pool and the pool life. So, before replying, Bart thinks of Lucy's lack of perception in words that are seemingly simple but which are, in effect, richly suggestive: 'Skimming the surface, she ignored the battle in the mud'(237). The play of ideas stems, in the main, from the resonating words 'surface' and 'mud'. Swallows skim the surface and are symbolic of Lucy. He, on the other hand, can understand Miss La Trobe because he knows the 'battle in the mud'. He sees at once what she needs: 'What she wanted, like that carp (something moved in the water) was darkness in the mud'(237). The need is entirely embodied in 'pool' references, the water, darkness, mud, carp, and is then glossed plainly as 'a whisky and soda at the pub'(238). The 'great carp himself' who seldom comes to the surface is, however, old Bart. This reference is picked up later

THE 'PURE POETRY' OF *BETWEEN THE ACTS*

when Lucy is talking to William Dodge; it expresses his oppressive dominance over her: 'It was always "my brother ... my brother" who rose from the depths of her lily pool' (241). There has therefore been a gradual movement from outer to inner: Lucy and old Bart, to begin with, stood by the pool; the pool has now become Lucy's consciousness.

In the course of the novel, then, there are various points at which several meanings come together. One such occurs when Lucy is left by herself at the side of the pool. Pointz Hall is, as we have noted, in the 'heart' of England. The Oliver family is a 'middle'-class family belonging neither to the old-established gentry nor to the newcomers to the village, but placed somewhere between the two. The pool is placed literally and symbolically between Pointz Hall and the Pageant. The audience and the actors in the Pageant recognized themselves as 'We. Ourselves'. Now, looking into the pool, Lucy suddenly has a final glimpse of 'Ourselves':

> "Ourselves," she murmured. And retrieving some glint of faith from the grey waters, hopefully, without much help from reason, she followed the fish; the speckled, streaked, and blotched; seeing in that vision beauty, power, and glory in ourselves.

> (239–40)

Finally, the image of the pool is used in a different sense in referring to Miss La Trobe. She is a seeker for the reality below the surface of life, an explorer of the depth:

> All this Miss La Trobe knew, but refused to be mixed up in it. She splashed into the fine mesh like a great stone into the lily pool. The criss-cross was shattered. Only the roots beneath water were of use to her.

> (79–80)

And the pool is also the creative unconscious from which inspiration for another play will rise and from which the Pageant had grown.

> Words of one syllable sank down into the mud. She drowsed; she nodded. The mud became fertile. Words rose....

> (247–8)

VIRGINIA WOOLF AND THE POETRY OF FICTION

Reflected in the pool, therefore, are both 'ourselves' and the Pageant.

It is, then, in the symbolic use of such places as the lily pool and the barn, and the clustering of key words and symbols, that the poetic core of this novel about a nation on the brink of war is to be found. Although much of the time it is the surface narrative of the novel that the reader is enagaged with, there is a rich substratum to be explored. It is to be found in the richness and density of the often hidden poetry of this novel. It is not the high mystical poetry of *The Waves* but the poetry of ordinary everyday existence. An entry in Virginia Woolf's diary seems to suggest this:

> The exact narrative of this last morning should refer to Louie's interruption, holding a glass jar, in whose thin milk was a pat of butter. Then I went in with her to skim the milk off: then I took the pat and showed it to Leonard. This was a moment of great household triumph.
>
> I am a little triumphant about the book [*Between the Acts*]. I think it's an interesting attempt in a new method. I think it's more quintessential than the others. More milk skimmed off. A richer pat....

(*AWD*: 359)

SELECT BIBLIOGRAPHY

For comprehensive bibliographies of Virginia Woolf criticism see Barbara Weiser (1972) 'Criticism of Virginia Woolf from 1956 to the present', *Modern Fiction Studies* XVIII Lafayette; Robin Majumdar (1976) *Virginia Woolf: An Annotated Bibliography of Criticism, 1915–1974*, New York: Garland. For a bibliography of the writings of Virginia Woolf see B. J. Kirkpatrick (1957) *A Bibliography of Virginia Woolf*, London: Rupert Hart-Davis.

VIRGINIA WOOLF'S PUBLISHED WORKS

Novels

Where there has been more than one edition, the first of the two publication dates is that of the first edition (published by the Hogarth Press unless stated to the contrary); the second that of the Hogarth Press Uniform Edition to which all references, with the exception of *Night and Day*, are made.

Woolf, Virginia (1915, 1949) *The Voyage Out*, London: Duckworth, Hogarth Press.

—— (1919) *Night and Day*, London: Duckworth.

—— (1922, 1971) *Jacob's Room.*

—— (1925, 1960) *Mrs. Dalloway.*

—— (1927, 1960) *To the Lighthouse.*

—— (1928) *Orlando.*

—— (1931, 1963) *The Waves.*

—— (1933) *Flush: A Biography.*

—— (1937) *The Years.*

—— (1941, 1965) *Between the Acts.*

SELECT BIBLIOGRAPHY

Other Works

Woolf, Virginia (1918) *The Pargiters: the Novel-Essay Portion of The Years*, ed. Mitchell A. Leaska, London: Hogarth Press.
—— (1925) *The Common Reader: First Series*, London: Hogarth Press.
—— (1929, 1977) *A Room of One's Own*, London: Hogarth Press; St Albans: Triad Panther.
—— (1932) *The Common Reader: Second Series*, London: Hogarth Press.
—— (1938, 1977) *Three Guineas*, London: Hogarth Press; Harmondsworth: Penguin.
—— (1940, 1979) *Roger Fry*, London: Hogarth Press; Harmondsworth: Penguin.
—— (1942) *The Death of the Moth and Other Essays*, London: Hogarth Press.
—— (1943) *A Haunted House and Other Stories*, London: Hogarth Press.
—— (1950) *The Captain's Death Bed and Other Essays*, London: Hogarth Press.
—— (1954, 1978) *A Writer's Diary*, ed. Leonard Woolf, London: Hogarth Press; St Albans: Triad.
—— (1958) *Granite and Rainbow*, London: Hogarth Press.
—— (1966) *Collected Essays*, 4 vols, London: Chatto & Windus.
—— (1973) *Mrs. Dalloway's Party*, ed. Stella McNichol, London: Hogarth Press.
—— (1976) *Moments of Being: Unpublished Autobiographical Writings*, ed. Jeanne Schulkind, Sussex: The University Press.
—— (1975–80, 1977–82) *The Letters of Virginia Woolf*, 6 vols, eds Nigel Nicolson and Joanne Trautman, London: Hogarth Press; Chatto & Windus.
—— (1977–83, 1979–85) *The Diary of Virginia Woolf*, 5 vols, ed. Anne Olivier Bell, London: Hogarth Press; Harmondsworth: Penguin.

BIOGRAPHICAL

(see also Letters and Diaries listed above)
Bell, Quentin (1968) *Bloomsbury*, London: Weidenfeld & Nicolson.
—— *Virginia Woolf: A Biography*, 2 vols, London: Hogarth Press, 1972; St Albans: Triad, 1976.
Gordon, Lyndall (1984) *Virginia Woolf*, Oxford: Oxford University Press.
Spater, George and Parsons, Ian (1960) *A Marriage of True Minds: an Intimate Portrait of Leonard and Virginia Woolf*, London: Jonathan Cape and Hogarth Press.

SELECT BIBLIOGRAPHY

Woolf, Leonard (1960) *Sowing: An Autobiography of the Years 1880–1904*, London: Hogarth Press.

— (1969) *Growing: an Autobiography of the Years 1904–1911*, London: Hogarth Press.

— (1964) *Beginning Again: an Autobiography of the Years 1911-1918*, London: Hogarth Press.

— (1967) *Downhill All the Way: an Autobiography of the Years 1919–1939*, London: Hogarth Press.

— (1969) *The Journey not the Arrival Matters: an Autobiography of the Years 1939–1969*, London: Hogarth Press.

These five volumes are also available as *An Autobiography*, Oxford: Oxford University Press, 1980.

GENERAL STUDIES OF VIRGINIA WOOLF; AND GENERAL STUDIES OF FICTION WITH SECTIONS THAT REFER TO VIRGINIA WOOLF

Auerbach, Erich (1953) *Mimesis: the Representation of Reality in Western Literature*, Princeton, NJ: Princeton University Press.

Bayley, John (1957, 1969) *The Romantic Survival: a Study in Poetic Evolution*, London: Constable, Chatto & Windus.

Bazin, Nancy Topping (1973) *Virginia Woolf and the Androgynous Vision*, New Brunswick, NJ: Rutgers University Press.

Beach, Joseph Warren (1932) *The Twentieth Century Novel: Studies in Technique*, New York: Appleton-Century-Crofts.

Bennett, Joan (1964) *Virginia Woolf: Her Art as a Novelist*, Cambridge: Cambridge University Press.

Blackstone, Bernard (1949) *Virginia Woolf: a Commentary*, London: Hogarth Press.

Brewster, Dorothy (1959) *Virginia Woolf's London*, London: Allen & Unwin.

— (1963) *Virginia Woolf*, London: Allen & Unwin.

Brower, Reuben Arthur (1951) *The Fields of Light: an Experiment in Critical Reading*, New York: Oxford University Press.

Cecil, David (1949) *Poets and Storytellers*, New York: Macmillan.

Chambers, R.L. (1947) *The Novels of Virginia Woolf*, Edinburgh: Oliver & Boyd.

Cohn, Dorrit (1978) *Transparent Minds: Narrative Modes for Presenting Consciousness in Fiction*, Princeton, NJ: Princeton University Press.

Cox, C.B. (1963) *The Free Spirit: a Study of Humanism in the Novels of George Eliot, Henry James, E. M. Forster, Virginia Woolf, Angus Wilson*, London: Oxford University Press.

Daiches, David (1960) *The Novel and the Modern World*, Chicago: University of Chicago Press.

SELECT BIBLIOGRAPHY

—— (1963) *Virginia Woolf*, New York: New Directions.

Edel, Leon (1964) *The Modern Psychological Novel*, New York: Grosset & Dunlap.

Fleishman, Avrom (1975) *Virginia Woolf, A Critical Reading*, Baltimore and London: Johns Hopkins University Press.

Freedman, Ralph (1963) *The Lyrical Novel: Studies in Hermann Hesse, André Gide, and Virginia Woolf*, Princeton, NJ: Princeton University Press.

Friedman, Melvin (1955) *Stream of Consciousness: A Study in Literary Method*, New Haven: Yale University Press.

Guiguet, Jean (1965) *Virginia Woolf and Her Works*, trans. Jean Stewart, London: Hogarth Press.

Hafley, James (1954) *The Glass Roof: Virginia Woolf as Novelist*, Berkeley: University of California Press.

Harper, Howard (1982) *Between Language and Silence*, Baton Rouge: Louisiana State University Press.

Johnstone, J.K. (1954) *The Bloomsbury Group: A Study of E.M.Forster, Lytton Strachey, Virginia Woolf, and Their Circle*, London: Secker & Warburg.

Kelley, Alice van Buren (1973) *The Novels of Virginia Woolf: Fact and Vision*, Chicago and London: University of Chicago Press.

Kettle, Arnold (1953) *An Introduction to the English Novel*, 2 vols, London: Hutchinson.

Leaska, Mitchell A. (1970) *Virginia Woolf's Lighthouse: a Study in Critical Method*, London: Columbia University Press.

—— (1979) *The Novels of Virginia Woolf: From Beginning to End*, London: Weidenfeld & Nicolson.

Lewis, Wyndham (1934) *Men without Art*, London: Cassel.

Love, Jean O. (1970) *Worlds in Consciousness: Mythopoetic Thought in the Novels of Virginia Woolf*, Berkeley: University of California Press.

McLaurin, Allen (1973) *Virginia Woolf: the Echoes Enslaved*, Cambridge: Cambridge University Press.

Marder, Herbert (1968) *Feminism and Art: A Study of Virginia Woolf*, Chicago: University of Chicago Press.

Minow-Pinknery, Makiko (1987) *Virginia Woolf and The Problem of the Subject: Feminine Writing in the Major Novels*, Brighton: Harvester.

Moody, A.D. (1963) *Virginia Woolf*, Edinburgh: Oliver & Boyd.

Moore, Madeline (1984) *The Short Season Between Two Silences*, Boston: Allen & Unwin.

Naremore, James (1973) *The World Without a Self: Virginia Woolf and the Novel*, New Haven and London: Yale University Press.

Poole, Roger (1978) *The Unknown Virginia Woolf*, Cambridge: Cambridge University Press.

Richter, Harvena (1970) *Virginia Woolf: The Inward Voyage*, Princeton, NJ: Princeton University Press.

SELECT BIBLIOGRAPHY

Rosenthal, Michael (1979) *Virginia Woolf*, London: Routledge & Kegan Paul.

Savage, D.S. (1950) *The Withered Branch: Six Studies in the Modern Novel*, London: Eyre & Spottiswoode.

Schaefer, Josephine O'Brien (1965) *The Three-fold Nature of Reality in the Novels of Virginia Woolf*, The Hague: Mouton.

Seward, Barbara (1960) *The Symbolic Rose*, New York: Columbia University Press.

Silver, Brenda R. (1983) *Virginia Woolf's Reading Notebooks*, Princeton, NJ: Princeton University Press.

Thakur, N.C. (1965) *The Symbolism of Virginia Woolf*, London: Oxford University Press.

Tindall, William York (1955) *The Literary Symbol*, New York: Columbia University Press.

ARTICLES

Aiken, Conrad (1927) 'The novel as a work of art', *Dial* 83 (July), pp. 41–4.

Batchelor, J.B. (1968) 'Feminism in Virginia Woolf', *English* 17, pp. 1–7.

Beach, Joseph Warren (1937) 'Virginia Woolf', *English Journal* 26 (October), pp. 603–12.

Beja, Morris (1964) 'Matches struck in the dark: Virginia Woolf's moments of vision', *Critical Quarterly* 6 (Summer), pp. 137–52.

Bradbrook, M.C. (1932) 'Notes on the style of Mrs Woolf', *Scrutiny* 1 (May), pp. 33–9.

Eliot, T.S. (1941) 'Virginia Woolf', *Horizon* 3 (May), pp. 313–16.

Gregor, Ian (1980) 'Voices: Reading Virginia Woolf', *Sewanee Review* 88, pp. 572–90.

Hasler, Jörg (1982) 'Virginia Woolf and the chimes of Big Ben', *English Studies* 63, pp. 145–58.

Hintikka, Jaakko (1979) 'Virginia Woolf and Our Knowledge of the external world', *Journal of Aesthetics and Art Criticism* 38, pp. 5–14.

Leavis, F.R. (1942) 'After "To the Lighthouse" ', *Scrutiny* 10 (January), pp. 295–8.

McLaughlin, Thomas M. (1981) 'Fiction and interpretation in Virginia Woolf', *Essays in Literature* 8, pp. 173–87.

Page, Alex (1961) 'A dangerous day: Mrs Dalloway discovers her double', *Modern Fiction Studies* 7 (Summer), pp. 115–24.

Roberts, John H. (1946) ' "Vision and Design" in Virginia Woolf', *PMLA* 61, pp. 835–47.

Simon, Irene (1960) 'Some aspects of Virginia Woolf's imagery', *English Studies* 41, pp. 180–96.

SELECT BIBLIOGRAPHY

Smart, J.A.E. (1941) 'Virginia Woolf', *Dalhousie Review* 21 (April), pp. 37–50.

OTHER WORKS

Bell, Clive (1931) *Art*, London: Chatto and Windus.
Fry, Roger (1928) *Vision and Design*, London: Chatto & Windus.
Mallarmé, Stéphane (1956) 'Crisis in Poetry', *Mallarmé: Selected Prose, Poems, Essays and Letters*, intro. and trans. Bradford Cook, Baltimore: Johns Hopkins University Press.

INDEX

Austen, Jane 16, 22

Bell, Clive 97
Bell, Vanessa 106
Bergson, Henri 4, 101
Bible 124, 130, 133
'Bloomsbury' 48
Browning, Robert xi

Dante 34
Depression, The xiii
Disney, Walt 170

Edwardian period xii, 1, 56
Eliot, T. S. 4, 52–3, 107

Fascism xiii, 145–7, 150
Forster, E. M. 17, 48
Fry, Roger 93–7, 106

Gibbon, Edward *The Decline and Fall of the Roman Empire* 14

Hardy, Thomas 95–6, 98

Ibsen, Henrik *A Doll's House* 2

James, Henry 11

Mallarmé, Stéphane 141, 168
Meredith, George xi, 2–3
Modernism xii, 1, 53
Murry, John Middleton 118

'New Woman' 1

Plato 59
Post-Impressionist exhibition of 1910 93, 106

Shakespeare, William xii, 16, 17, 22–5, 26, 30, 31, 34, 36, 37, 40, 88–9
Sidney, Philip 26
Stephen, Julius Thoby 48
Stephen, Leslie 92, 95, 96, 106
Sterne, Laurence *Tristram Shandy* 94

Victorian period 1, 161

War of 1914–18 xii, 52, 56, 58–61, 98, 106, 110–11, 116
War of 1939–45 xiii, 143–7, 154
Wells, H. G. *The Outline of History* 149
Wilcox, Mrs in E. M. Forster's *Howards End* 17
Wilde, Oscar xi
Woolf, Leonard 48, 143
Woolf, Virginia
    A Room of One's Own 62–3, 66, 78
    'A Sketch of the Past' 117, 119, 123–5, 129, 133, 140, 151
    A Writer's Diary 92–3, 95–6, 118, 119–22, 141, 143–4, 145–6, 174
    Between the Acts xii, xiii, 141–7
    Jacob's Room xii, 39–61, 91, 93, 97, 99, 118
    'Modern Fiction' xii, 48
    Mrs. Dalloway xii, 4, 39–40, 62–90, 91, 94, 118, 151
    Night and Day xii, 16–38, 39, 91, 142

INDEX

'On Not Knowing Greek' 57
The Voyage Out xi, 1–15, 16, 17, 39,
42, 91
The Waves xii, xiii, 5, 117–40, 141,
142, 151, 174
The Years xiii, 141, 143, 146–8
To the Lighthouse xii, 5, 17, 39, 41–
2, 91–116, 117, 118, 119, 120, 122,
123, 124
Wordsworth, William 162

Yeats, William Butler 110